new interchange

Jack C. Richards
Chuck Sandy

video teacher's guide

1

CAMBRIDGE
UNIVERSITY PRESS

Revised for use with *New Interchange*

PUBLISHED BY THE PRESS SYNDICATE OF THE UNIVERSITY OF CAMBRIDGE
The Pitt Building, Trumpington Street, Cambridge, United Kingdom

CAMBRIDGE UNIVERSITY PRESS
The Edinburgh Building, Cambridge CB2 2RU, UK
40 West 20th Street, New York, NY 10011–4211, USA
477 Williamstown Road, Port Melbourne, VIC 3207, Australia
Ruiz de Alarcón 13, 28014 Madrid, Spain
Dock House, The Waterfront, Cape Town 8001, South Africa

http://www.cambridge.org

© Cambridge University Press 1994, 1998

First published 1994
Second edition 1998
4th printing 2002

Printed in the United States of America

Typeface New Century Schoolbook   System QuarkXPress®   [AH]

ISBN 0 521 62881 4 Student's Book 1
ISBN 0 521 62880 6 Student's Book 1A
ISBN 0 521 62879 2 Student's Book 1B
ISBN 0 521 62878 4 Workbook 1
ISBN 0 521 62877 6 Workbook 1A
ISBN 0 521 62876 8 Workbook 1B
ISBN 0 521 62875 X Teacher's Edition 1
ISBN 0 521 62874 1 Teacher's Manual 1
ISBN 0 521 62873 3 Class Audio Cassettes 1
ISBN 0 521 62871 7 Student's Audio Cassette 1A
ISBN 0 521 62869 5 Student's Audio Cassette 1B
ISBN 0 521 62872 5 Class Audio CDs 1
ISBN 0 521 62870 9 Student's Audio CD 1A
ISBN 0 521 62868 7 Student's Audio CD 1B
ISBN 0 521 95019 8 Audio Sampler 1–3

Also available
ISBN 0 521 62867 9 Video 1 (NTSC)
ISBN 0 521 62866 0 Video 1 (PAL)
ISBN 0 521 62865 2 Video 1 (SECAM)
ISBN 0 521 62864 4 Video Activity Book 1
ISBN 0 521 62863 6 Video Teacher's Guide 1
ISBN 0 521 63887 9 Video Sampler 1–2
ISBN 0 521 62667 6 CD-ROM (PC format)
ISBN 0 521 62666 8 CD-ROM (Mac format)
ISBN 0 521 77381 4 Lab Guide 1
ISBN 0 521 77380 6 Lab Cassettes 1
ISBN 0 521 46759 4 Placement Test (valid for New
                    Interchange and Interchange)
ISBN 0 521 80575 9 Teacher-Training Video with
                    Video Manual

Forthcoming
ISBN 0 521 62882 2 New Interchange/Passages
                    Placement and Evaluation
                    Package

Book design, art direction, and layout services: Adventure House, NYC

Contents

Plan of Video 1

Introduction

NEW INTERCHANGE

New Interchange is a revision of *Interchange,* one of the world's most successful and popular English courses. *New Interchange* is a multi-level course in English as a second or foreign language for young adults and adults. The course covers the four skills of listening, speaking, reading, and writing, as well as improving pronunciation and building vocabulary. Particular emphasis is placed on listening and speaking. The primary goal of the course is to teach communicative competence, that is, the ability to communicate in English according to the situation, purpose, and roles of the participants. The language used in *New Interchange* is American English; however, the course reflects the fact that English is the major language of international communication and is not limited to any one country, region, or culture. Level One is for students at the beginner or false-beginner level.

Level One builds on the foundations for accurate and fluent communication already established in the Intro Level by extending grammatical, lexical, and functional skills. The syllabus covered in Level One also incorporates a rapid review of language from the Intro Level, allowing Student's Book 1 to be used with students who have not studied with Intro.

THE VIDEO COURSE

New Interchange Video 1 has been revised for use with *New Interchange*. The Video is designed to complement the Student's Book or to be used independently as the basis for a short listening and speaking course.

As a complement to the Student's Book, the Video provides a variety of entertaining and instructive live-action sequences. Each video sequence provides further practice related to the topics, language, and vocabulary introduced in the corresponding unit of the Student's Book.

As the basis for a short, free-standing course, the Video serves as an exciting vehicle for introducing and practicing useful conversational language used in everyday situations.

The Video Activity Book contains a wealth of activities that reinforce and extend the content of the Video, whether it is used to supplement the Student's Book or as the basis for an independent course. The Video Teacher's Guide provides thorough support for both situations.

COURSE LENGTH

The Video contains sixteen dramatized sequences and five documentary sequences. These vary slightly in length, but in general, the sequences are approximately three minutes each, and the documentaries are approximately five minutes each.

The accompanying units in the Video Activity Book are designed for maximum flexibility and provide anywhere from 45 to 90 minutes of classroom activity. Optional activities described in the Video Teacher's Guide may be used to extend the lesson as needed.

MORE ABOUT THE COURSE COMPONENTS

Video

The sixteen dramatized video sequences complement Units 1 through 16 of *New Interchange* Student's Book 1. Although each sequence is linked to the topic of the corresponding Student's Book unit, it presents a new situation and introduces characters who do not appear in the text. This element of diversity helps keep students' interest high and also allows the Video to be used effectively as a free-standing course. At the same time, the language used in the video sequences reflects the structures and vocabulary of the Student's Book, which is based on an integrated syllabus that links grammar and communicative functions.

The five documentaries may be used for review or at any point in the course. These sequences correspond to the placement of the review units in the Student's Book, with a fifth "bonus" documentary appearing after Sequence 2. The documentaries are based on authentic, unscripted interviews with people in various situations, and serve to illustrate how language is used by real people in real situations.

Video Activity Book

The Video Activity Book contains sixteen units based on live-action sequences and five documentary units that correspond to the video sequences and documentaries, and is designed to facilitate the effective use of the Video in the classroom. Each unit includes previewing, viewing, and postviewing activities that provide learners with step-by-step support and guidance in understanding and working with the events and language of the sequence. Learners expand their cultural awareness, develop skills and strategies for communicating effectively, and use language creatively.

Video Teacher's Guide

The Video Teacher's Guide contains detailed suggestions for how to use the Video and the Video Activity Book in the classroom, and includes an overview of video teaching techniques, unit-by-unit notes, and a range of optional extension activities. The Video Teacher's Guide also includes answers to the activities in the Video Activity Book and photocopiable transcripts of the video sequences.

■ VIDEO IN THE CLASSROOM

The use of video in the classroom can be an exciting and effective way to teach and learn. As a medium, video both motivates and entertains students. The *New Interchange* Video is a unique resource that does the following:

- Depicts dynamic, natural contexts for language use.
- Presents authentic language as well as cultural information about speakers of English through engaging story lines.

- Enables learners to use visual information to enhance comprehension.
- Focuses on the important cultural dimension of learning a language by actually showing how speakers of the language live and behave.
- Allows learners to observe the gestures, facial expressions, and other aspects of body language that accompany speech.

■ WHAT EACH UNIT OF THE VIDEO ACTIVITY BOOK CONTAINS

Each unit of the Video Activity Book is divided into four sections: *Preview*, *Watch the Video*, *Follow-up*, and *Language Close-up*. In general, these four sections include, but are not limited to, the following types of activities:

Preview

Culture The culture previews introduce the topics of the video sequences and provide important background and cultural information. They can be presented in class as reading and discussion activities, or students can read and complete them as homework.

Vocabulary The vocabulary activities introduce and practice the essential vocabulary of the video sequences through a variety of interesting tasks.

Guess the Story/Guess the Facts The Guess the Story (or in some units Guess the Facts) activities allow students to make predictions about characters and their actions by watching the video sequences without the sound or by looking at photos in the Video Activity Book. These schema-building activities help to improve students' comprehension when they watch the sequences with the sound.

Watch the Video

Get the Picture These initial viewing activities help students gain global understanding of the sequences by focusing on gist. Activity types vary from unit to unit, but typically involve watching for key information needed to complete a chart, answer questions, or put events in order.

Watch for Details In these activities, students focus on more detailed meaning by watching and listening for specific information to complete tasks about the story line and the characters.

What's Your Opinion? In these activities, students respond to the sequences by making inferences about the characters' actions, feelings, and motivations, and by stating their opinions about issues and topics.

Follow-up

Role Play, Interview, and Other Expansion Activities This section includes communicative activities based on the sequences in which students extend and personalize what they have learned.

Language Close-up

What Did They Say? These cloze activities focus on the specific language in the sequences by having students watch and listen in order to fill in missing words in conversations.

Grammar and Functional Activities In these activities, which are titled to reflect the structural and functional focus of a particular unit, students practice, in a meaningful way, the grammatical structures and functions presented in the video sequences.

GUIDELINES FOR TEACHING THE NEW INTERCHANGE VIDEO

The Course Philosophy

The philosophy underlying *New Interchange* is that learning a second or foreign language is more meaningful and effective when the language is used for real communication instead of being studied as an end in itself. The *New Interchange* Video and Video Activity Book provide a multi-skills syllabus in which each element in the course is linked.

In the Video Activity Book, for example, the Preview activities build on each other to provide students with relevant background information and key vocabulary that will assist them in better understanding a video sequence. These activities give students the tools for developing essential *top-down processing skills,* the process by which students use background knowledge and relevant information about the situation, context, and topic along with key words and predicting strategies to arrive at comprehension.

The carefully sequenced Watch the Video activities first help students focus on gist and then guide them in identifying important details and language. In addition to assisting students in understanding the sequence, these tasks also prepare them for Follow-up speaking activities, which encourage students to extend and personalize information by voicing their opinions or carrying out communicative tasks.

To conclude students' work with the video sequence, many of the Language Close-up activities focus on developing *bottom-up processing skills,* which require students to decode individual words in a message to derive meaning. The combination of top-down and bottom-up processing skills allows students to understand the general story line of a sequence and the specific language used to tell the story.

Options for the Classroom

The Video Teacher's Guide provides step-by-step instructions for all of the activities in the Video Activity Book. Teachers should not think, however, that there is a limited number of ways to present the material. Most activities can be carried out in a number of ways, and teachers are strongly encouraged to experiment, taking into account the proficiency levels and needs of their students as they plan lessons based on the Video.

Although the procedures for many of the Watch the Video activities state that students should keep their books open while viewing, teachers should feel free to have students try some of these types of activities with their books closed. Likewise, a similar suggestion holds true for other activities that the Video Teacher's Guide suggests be done with books closed – students may benefit from trying certain of these activities with their books open.

The richness of video as a learning medium provides teachers with many options for the classroom. Each lesson in the Video Teacher's Guide describes several classroom-tested activities to extend each sequence and documentary. However, teachers should again note that these suggested activities cover only a few of the many possibilities. Teachers are encouraged to use the Video as a springboard for further classroom activities appropriate to their teaching and learning situations.

General Video Techniques to Try

Once teachers feel comfortable with the basic course procedures, they are encouraged to experiment with other effective – and enjoyable – classroom techniques for presenting and working with the video. Here are several proven techniques.

Fast-Forward Viewing For activities in which students watch the video sequence with the sound off, play the entire sequence on fast-forward and have students list all of the things that they can see. For example, for *Documentary 1: Jobs*, have students watch the sequence in fast-forward and list all of the jobs they see people doing. Nearly all of the activities designed to be completed with the sound off can be done in this manner.

Information Gap Play approximately the first half of a sequence, and then stop the video. Have students work in pairs or groups to predict what is going to happen next. For example, in *Unit 9: Help is coming*, stop the video sequence just before the two men walk up the driveway. Ask students, "Who are these men?" Have students predict the answer, and then play the rest of the sequence so that students can check their predictions.

The procedure for another information-gap activity is as follows: Have half of the students in the class leave the room or turn their backs to the video monitor while the rest of the students view the sequence. Then give the students who have viewed the sequence the task of explaining the basic story line to those who have not seen the sequence. This can be done as a pair, small-group, or class activity.

Act It Out All of the video sequences and documentaries provide an excellent basis for role plays and drama activities. Try this procedure: Select a short scene, and have students watch it several times. Then have pairs or groups act out the scene, staying as close as possible to the actions and expressions of the characters. Have pairs or groups act out their scenes in front of the class.

Slow Viewing Have students watch a sequence or documentary played in slow motion. As they view, have students call out all of the things they can see people doing or wearing or eating – whatever is appropriate to a particular unit.

What Are They Saying? Have students watch a short segment of a sequence in which two people are talking, but with the sound off. Then have students, working in pairs, use the context to predict what the people might be saying to each other. Have pairs write out sample dialogues, and then share their work with the class.

Freeze-Frame Freeze a frame of a sequence or documentary, and have students call out information about the scene. For example, have students tell about the objects they can see, about what the people are doing, about the time and place – whatever is appropriate to the scene or their learning situation.

■ HOW TO TEACH A TYPICAL NEW INTERCHANGE VIDEO SEQUENCE

The unit-by-unit notes in the Video Teacher's Guide give detailed suggestions for teaching each unit. In addition to these comprehensive notes, here is a set of procedures that can be used to teach any of the units of the *New Interchange* Video.

First, introduce the topic of the unit by asking questions and eliciting information from the students related to the theme of the unit. Then, explain what the students will study (e.g., mention the main topics, functions, and structures), and set the scene. Give students an indication of what they will see in the video sequence. Next, present the activities and tasks using the following guidelines.

Preview

Culture

- Books closed. Introduce the topic by asking questions about it. Use these questions to elicit or present the key vocabulary items and to provide background knowledge on the topic of the culture reading. If possible, ask questions that can be answered by reading the text.
- Books open. Have students read the text and check predictions. Teachers may want students to circle no more than three key vocabulary items for which they require definitions.
- Lead the students through the information in the text. Go over any comprehension problems and questions as they arise. Answer any vocabulary questions that still exist.
- Have students complete the task individually or in pairs.
- Have students compare answers with a partner or around the class.

As an alternative, follow this procedure:

- Ask students to read the culture information at home, referring to a dictionary as necessary, and answer the accompanying questions before class.
- Have students compare answers with a partner in class.

In general, teachers should always feel free to provide additional related culture information as appropriate and available.

Vocabulary

- Introduce and model the pronunciation of the words in the activity.
- Have students complete the task in pairs or individually.
- Have students compare answers with a partner or around the class.
- Check students' answers.
- Encourage students to supply additional related vocabulary items where appropriate.

Guess the Story/Guess the Facts

- Ask students to think about the topic of the unit and look at the photos in order to guess what the video sequence is about. Accept all answers at this stage.

- Explain the task, and lead students through the procedure. Answer any questions that arise.
- Play the video sequence with the sound off.
- Have students complete the task individually or in pairs.
- Have students check their predictions and compare answers with a partner or around the class.
- Check students' answers.
- Replay appropriate portions of the video sequence as needed.

Watch the Video

Get the Picture

- Direct students' attention to the task, and read through it with them. Answer vocabulary or procedural questions as they arise.
- Have students work alone and predict answers to questions if they feel they have enough information to do so.
- Remind students that this is a gist activity and that they do not need to try to understand every detail in the sequence. Encourage students to stay focused on the task.
- Play the entire video sequence with the sound on. Replay if necessary.
- Have students complete the task individually or in pairs. When appropriate, have them check the predictions they made in Guess the Story/Guess the Facts as well.
- Have students compare answers with a partner or around the class.
- If time permits, have students check answers while watching the video sequence again.
- Check students' answers.

Watch for Details

- Explain the task. Lead students through the instructions and questions.
- Answer any vocabulary and procedural questions that arise.
- Play the entire video sequence with the sound on. Replay as necessary.
- Have students complete the task individually or in pairs.

- Have students compare answers with a partner or around the class.
- If time permits, have students check their answers while watching the sequence again.
- Check students' answers.

Follow-up
Role Play, Interview, and Other Expansion Activities

Note that since each activity in this section gives students the opportunity to extend and personalize what they have learned in the video sequence and the Video Activity Book, encourage students to use new language to talk about themselves and their ideas as they complete the tasks.

- Explain the task. Lead students through the procedure. Answer vocabulary and procedural questions as they arise.
- Have students complete the task individually, in pairs, or in small groups as noted in the unit instructions.
- Have students compare answers in pairs or in small groups.
- When appropriate, have selected pairs or groups act out the activity for the class.

Language Close-up
What Did They Say?

- Lead students through the task instructions. Answer procedural questions as necessary.
- Have students read the cloze conversation and predict answers when possible.
- Play the appropriate section of the video sequence, and do a spot-check to gauge overall comprehension. Do not supply answers at this stage.
- Play the appropriate section of the video again. Have students compare answers with a partner or around the class.
- Ask if anyone would like to watch the video sequence again. Replay as necessary.
- Go over answers with the class, and discuss any trouble spots.
- If you wish, divide the class in half or in groups, and lead a choral repetition and practice of the cloze conversation.

- When students are comfortable with the dialogue, have them practice it in pairs or small groups, depending on the number of characters required.
- Have selected pairs or groups read or act out the dialogue for the class.

Grammar and Functional Activities

These activities vary from unit to unit, depending on the particular structural and functional focus of a given unit. In general, though, teachers can follow these procedures.

- Present the grammatical structure, and give example sentences from the video script or from students' experiences.
- Lead students through the task, and answer vocabulary and procedural questions as needed.
- Have students complete the task individually or in pairs.
- Have students compare answers with a partner or around the class.
- Check students' answers.
- Review the grammatical structure as appropriate.
- Teachers using *New Interchange* Student's Book 1 should refer students back to the grammar focus in the appropriate unit as necessary.

Optional Activities

The detailed notes for each unit give several optional activities that build on the topic, content, and structural focus of that unit. Teachers are encouraged to select from these suggested activities and use them in class as time permits.

The richness of the visual context leaves additional room for teachers to design and use their own extension activities in class when time is not an issue. Teachers are encouraged to do so.

A Final Note

These suggestions do not represent all of the possibilities for presenting and extending the material in the *New Interchange* Video or the Video Activity Book. Rather, they represent a wide sampling of well-tested activities that teachers are encouraged to use, adapt, modify, and extend to suit the particular needs of their students.

1 — First day at class

Topics/functions: Introducing oneself; addressing people (titles)

Structures: Yes/No and Wh-questions with *be*

Summary

The sequence takes place on the first day of class at a university. Marie Ouellette, a business management instructor, is in the hall outside her classroom talking to Sachiko Tanaka, one of her new students. Marie is checking the spelling of Sachiko's name in her class list when Rick, a student at the university, comes up to her. As Rick introduces himself and asks Marie questions, it is clear that he thinks she is a student. Later Rick realizes that Marie is not only a teacher at the university, but also the teacher of his next class. The sequence ends with an embarrassed Rick entering the classroom.

 *Preview*

1 CULTURE

The culture preview in the Video Activity Book teaches students some common ways to greet people in the United States and Canada. In universities, students generally use titles and last names when addressing their teachers, although in some schools, students may use first names. Titles are not used with first names in English. It is correct to say "Hello, Professor Lucas" or "Hello, Anne," but not "Hello, Professor Anne."

■ Books closed. Write your name on the board, and label your first and last name. Then label any other names you may have. If appropriate, explain that your friends call you by your first name and that your students call you by a title plus your last name.

■ Ask a few students to say their first names. Have others say their last names. Ask if anyone has a middle name or any other additional names.

■ Books open. Have the students read the culture information about names silently. Then answer any questions about vocabulary or content.

■ Read the questions, and have students work in small groups to answer them.

■ Check answers around the class.

Optional activity

Books closed. Introduce students to other titles (e.g., Mr., Mrs., Ms., Miss, Dr.). Write the names of some school officials on the board, and have students role-play introductions with the appropriate titles. (5 minutes)

2 VOCABULARY Nationalities

This activity introduces the names of the countries and nationalities presented in the video.

■ Books open. Read the instructions, and point out the example. Give additional examples if necessary.

■ *Pair work* Have students work together to complete the chart. (As an alternative, you may wish to have them work alone and then compare answers with a partner.) If time permits, encourage them to add additional countries and nationalities to the chart.

■ Check answers around the class.

Answers

Country	Nationality
Brazil	Brazilian
Canada	Canadian
England	English
France	French
Japan	Japanese
Korea	Korean
Mexico	Mexican
Spain	Spanish
Thailand	Thai

(see next page for an optional activity)

Optional activity

Pair work Books open. Have students classify nationalities into three groups: those that end in -*ish,* those that end in -*an,* and those that appear to be irregular. Then have them add two or three additional nationalities to each group. (5 minutes)

3 GUESS THE STORY

In this activity, students prepare to watch the sequence by making predictions about it based on visual information.

■ Books open. Have students look at the photo of Rick. Say, "This is Rick. How old is he? Can you guess?" Ask several students to guess, and accept all answers. Follow the same procedure for "What does Rick do?"

■ Books closed. Tell students to look at the video screen. Say, "Now, I will play the beginning of the video with no sound. After we watch, I will ask you again about Rick's age and his job."

■ Play the first minute of the sequence with the sound off (until just after Rick begins talking to Marie).

■ Ask students, "Now, about how old is Rick? What does he do?" Students should be able to make a good guess about Rick's age and say that he is in college.

■ Books open. Read through the task with students, and have them lightly check in their books which of the three possible answers they think is correct. Do not tell them the answer at this point. (He meets the teacher of his class.)

Optional activities

A Books closed. Play the first minute of the sequence with the sound off again. Then have students guess where Rick is, the season of the year, and the time of day. Accept all guesses if students can provide logical reasons for them. (5 minutes)

Possible answers

Rick is at his college/university. (He is carrying a book. There is a bookstore. There are many other students around. There are classrooms in the building.)

It is autumn./It is winter. (Rick is wearing a warm coat. Other students are wearing warm coats. There is no snow on the ground, so maybe it's autumn. A new class is beginning, so it is probably the fall or winter semester.)

It is in the morning or afternoon. (The sun is shining brightly.)

B **Pair work** Books closed. Play the first minute with the sound off once again. Have students work in pairs to list the things Rick does before he talks to Marie. (5 minutes)

Answers

Rick gets out of his car; he goes up the steps and enters the building; he buys a book in the bookstore; he walks to his classroom.

C **Pair work** Books closed. Have students work in pairs to guess what Rick says to Marie when he talks to her. Then have them write down their conversation. (5 minutes)

Possible conversation

Rick: Hello, my name is Rick.
Marie: Hello, Rick. It's nice to meet you. My name is Marie.
Rick: Nice to meet you, too, Marie. Are you a student here? . . .

D **Group work** Books closed. Have students compare the campus in the sequence with the place where they are studying by making a list with two columns ("The video" and "Our school") and listing similarities and differences. (5 minutes)

Watch the video

4 GET THE PICTURE

In this activity, students watch and listen only for the characters' names and occupations. You may wish to explain that *get the picture* is an idiom that means "understand the main idea or point of something."

■ Books open. Explain the activity, and tell students that they need to watch and listen only for people's names and occupations. Explain that they will listen again later for other information.

■ Play the sequence with the sound on. Tell students to complete the task while watching and then compare answers with a partner.

■ Check students' work, and show the sequence again if they are unsure of the answers.

Answers

Sachiko	Marie	Rick
Tanaka	Ouellette	?
student	teacher	student

5 WATCH FOR DETAILS

In this activity, students focus more closely on details by watching and listening for specific information about Rick, Marie, and Sachiko.

■ Books open. Explain the activity, and read through the items, answering any questions about vocabulary.

■ Books closed. Play the sequence with the sound on.

■ Books open. Have students complete the task alone and then compare answers with a partner.

■ Ask if anyone needs to watch the sequence again. Replay as needed, and then check answers.

Answers
1) Mexico
2) the United States
3) Canada
4) business management
5) business management

6 FORMS OF ADDRESS

This activity focuses on the various ways people address each other in English.

■ Books open. Explain the task. Refer students back to the culture preview on page 2 of the Video Activity Book to review some rules for addressing people in English.

■ Play the sequence with the sound on. Tell students to complete the task while watching and then compare answers with a partner.

■ Play the sequence again as needed, rather than giving answers.

Answers
1) Marie to Sachiko: title and last name/first name only
2) Marie to Rick: first name only
3) Rick to Marie: first name only
4) Sachiko to Marie: title and last name

Optional activities

A Books open. Refer students back to the culture preview. Have students compare the forms of address in the sequence to the ones they use in their own countries. (5 minutes)

B Books open or closed. Ask students if any of the speakers use the wrong form of address. If so, who? Why is it a mistake? (Rick calls Marie by her first name. He thinks she's a student.) (5 minutes)

7 WHAT'S YOUR OPINION?

In this activity, students give opinions about Rick's behavior. The Video Activity Book teaches some new adjectives students can use to describe Rick's and Marie's feelings.

- Books open. Explain the task, and lead students through the questions. Answer any vocabulary and comprehension questions.

- Have students complete the task alone or in pairs and then compare answers with a partner.

- Compare answers as a class.

Possible answers
1) to make a friend
2) embarrassed
3) amused

Optional activities

A Books open. Have students watch the sequence again with the sound off to look for visual information such as gestures, facial expressions, and actions that explain their choice of adjectives to describe the characters.

- Have students take turns describing the characters' feelings and imitating their gestures for the class. (5 minutes)

Possible answer
Rick is embarrassed. He looks down as he enters the classroom. (Student imitates Rick entering class with head down.)

B *Pair work* Books open. Have students list additional adjectives to describe Rick and Marie. (5 minutes)

Possible answers
Rick: friendly, talkative, polite
Marie: friendly, patient

 Follow-up

8 ROLE PLAY Meeting people

The first activity encourages students to be creative by having them play the roles of Rick, Sachiko, and Professor Ouellette. In the second activity, students introduce themselves, using their own information.

A *Group work* Books open. Explain the task, and put students in groups of three. Tell them that one student in each group should take the role of Rick, one student should take the role of Sachiko, and one the role of Professor Ouellette. As students write questions, remind them to write questions as Rick, Sachiko, or Professor Ouellette, and encourage them to be creative.

- Move around the room, and provide help as needed. Ask a few group members to share some questions with the class.

Possible questions
Professor Ouellette: Are you a student here? Are you taking business management?
Rick: Are you in this class?
Sachiko: What are you studying?

B Books open. Have students introduce themselves and have conversations within their groups. To extend this activity, you might have students mingle as if it's the first day of school and class has just ended. Tell them to introduce themselves and ask their questions to at least three additional people.

Optional activities

A Books open. Ask students which questions were the most interesting. Have each group choose their best question, and ask the questions around class. (5 minutes)

B Books closed. Have students watch the sequence and list all of the questions Rick asks Marie. (5 minutes)

Possible answers
Where are you from, Marie?
Oh, so you're Canadian?
From what city?
How about you? Are you a student, too?
Oh, what do you teach?

Language close-up

9 *WHAT DID THEY SAY?*

This cloze activity develops bottom-up listening skills by having students complete the first part of the conversation in the video.

■ Books open. Have students, working individually or in pairs, fill in any blanks they can before watching.

■ Play this segment of the sequence as many times as necessary while students work alone to fill in the blanks and check their predictions.

■ Have students compare answers with a partner and then watch again to check their answers.

■ Model the conversation or, if you wish, do choral or individual repetition to prepare for pair work. Then have students practice the conversation in pairs.

Answers

Rick: Hi. **My** name's Ricardo, but everybody calls me **Rick**.

Marie: Well, nice to **meet** you, Rick. **I'm** Marie Ouellette.

Rick: It's nice to meet you, Marie. . . . Um, **where** are you from, Marie?

Marie: I'm from **Canada**.

Rick: Oh, so **you're** Canadian?

Marie: That's right.

Rick: From what **city**?

Marie: Montreal. How **about** you?

Rick: I'm originally **from** Mexico City, but my family and I **live** up here **now**.

Marie: Oh, are you a **student** here?

Rick: Yes, I **am**.

Optional activities

A *Pair work* Books open. Have pairs act out the conversation, using as many of the characters' gestures, movements, and facial expressions as possible. (10 minutes)

B *Pair work* Books open. Have pairs act out the conversation again, substituting information of their own in the blanks. (5 minutes)

10 *QUESTIONS WITH* BE

In the first activity, students practice using the present tense of *be* in yes/no questions, one of the grammatical focuses of the sequence. In the second activity, students have the chance to ask and answer the questions.

A Books open. Explain the task, and go over the example. Provide additional examples of the structure if necessary.

■ Have the students fill in the correct forms of *be* in the questions and then compare answers with a partner.

B *Pair work* Books open. Have the students take turns asking and answering the questions. Move around the room checking for proper form. (Note: If students are not sure of an answer, you may replay the video rather than supply it.)

Answers to Activities 1 and 2

1) Is Miss Tanaka's first name Naomi?
   No, it isn't. It's Sachiko.
2) Are Rick and Sachiko students?
   Yes, they are.
3) Are you Canadian, Marie?
   Yes, I am.
4) Is Rick from Argentina?
   No, he isn't. He's from Mexico.
5) Are you a student here, Rick?
   Yes, I am.

Optional activity

Have students watch the sequence and list all of the yes/no questions with *be* that they hear. (7–10 minutes)

Answers

So you're Canadian? (Rick to Marie)
Oh, are you a student here? (Marie to Rick)
Are you a student, too? (Rick to Marie)
This is our classroom, isn't it? (Sachiko to Marie)

11 WH-QUESTIONS *Getting to know people*

In these activities students practice forming, asking, and answering Wh-questions, the second grammatical focus of the sequence.

A and **B** Books open. Follow the same procedures outlined for Exercise 10, "Questions with *be*."

Answers to Activities 1 and 2:

1) What is Sachiko's last name?
   Tanaka
2) Where are Rick and Sachiko from?
   Rick is from Mexico. Sachiko is (probably) from Japan.
3) What do you teach, Professor Ouellette?
   Business management.
4) What is Rick studying?
   Business management.
5) What do you do, Rick?
   I'm a student.

C *Class activity* Books open. Explain the task, and review the example.

■ Have students, working individually or in pairs, write additional questions. Encourage students to write Wh-questions. As students work, circulate to check for accuracy.

■ Have students stand and walk around, asking and answering questions with as many classmates as possible.

Possible questions
What's your name?
Where do you live?
Where are you from?
What do you do?
What do you study?

Optional activity

Have students watch the sequence and list all of the Wh-questions with *be* that they hear.
(7–10 minutes)

Answers
What's your first name again? (Marie to Sachiko)
Where are you from, Marie? (Rick to Marie)
What are you studying? (Marie to Rick)
So, what do you do? (Rick to Marie)
Oh, what do you teach? (Rick to Marie)

2 I need a change!

Topics/functions: Greetings and
introductions; talking about work

Structures: Wh-questions with *do;*
prepositions: *at, in,* and *to*

Summary

The sequence opens with Lynn Parker in her
office at AdTech, a computer software company
where she is a customer service manager. She
looks busy and overworked. The scene shifts to a
cafeteria-style restaurant. Lynn is looking for a
place to sit when her friend Paula greets her from
a nearby table. Lynn sits down and then
introduces herself to Bob, who is with Paula.
When Paula asks how everything is, Lynn
complains about her job. She explains that she
really wants to work in a hotel and is taking hotel
management classes in the evening. Bob says he
has a friend who manages a hotel in Hawaii and
implies that he might be able to help her get a job
there. The sequence ends with Lynn daydreaming
about a beach in Hawaii.

Preview

1 CULTURE

In the United States and Canada, colleges and
universities frequently offer evening and
Saturday classes for people who work full-time
but want to prepare for new careers. The culture
preview in the Video Activity Book gives more
information about work habits and career
patterns in the United States and Canada.

■ Books closed. To help students prepare to read
the culture preview, write the following questions
on the board (these questions are not given in the
Video Activity Book). Answer any questions about
vocabulary or content. For your reference, the
answers are given in parentheses.
1) In the United States and Canada, what
   time do you think people usually begin
   work? (9:00 A.M.)

2) What time do they usually finish
   work? (5:00 P.M.)
3) Do people in offices and businesses sometimes
   work late? (Yes.)
4) Do they get paid extra when they work
   late? (No.)
5) Do people in the United States and Canada
   often change jobs? (Yes.)

■ Have students work in pairs to discuss the
answers. Encourage them to make reasonable
guesses. (As an alternative, ask the questions to
the entire class and have students volunteer
their opinions.)

■ Ask students to share their answers with the
class. Encourage different answers but do not
give the correct answers at this point.

■ Books open. Have students read the culture
preview silently to check their predictions and
find the correct answers. Then review the
answers with the class.

■ Go over the questions, and then divide students
into small groups to discuss the answers.

■ Have groups report answers to the class.

2 VOCABULARY Occupations

This activity introduces the names of various jobs
at hotels and offices, the two workplaces talked
about in the sequence.

■ Books closed. Ask students to call out the names
of jobs of people who work in hotels, and write
the jobs on the board. Follow the same procedure
for jobs of people who work in offices.

■ Books open. Have students check to see if any
of the jobs they named are pictured. Go over
the jobs listed, and ask students to describe
the pictures.

■ *Pair work* Read the instructions, and go over
the examples. Have students work together to
complete the chart and then compare answers
with another pair.

(procedure continues on next page)

■ Check answers around the class. Ask students to call out the names of the additional jobs they listed. Confirm answers by writing them on the board.

Answers

Hotel	*Office*
bellhop	computer programmer
cashier	office manager
chef	secretary
secretary	

Additional jobs

Hotel	*Office*
salesclerk	clerk
waiter/waitress	receptionist
supervisor	supervisor

Optional activity

Books open. Have students work alone or in pairs to choose one job from each column and list some of its duties (e.g., cashier: greet people, count money, make change). (5 minutes)

3 GUESS THE STORY

In this activity, students prepare to watch the sequence by making predictions about Lynn's job based on visual information.

■ Books open. Have students look at the three photos. Read the questions, and then have students work individually or in pairs to guess the answers.

■ Have students report their predictions to the class, and accept all answers at this point.

■ Books closed. Tell students they will watch the beginning of the video sequence without sound, to get more information for making predictions about Lynn's job.

■ Play the opening scenes (until Lynn is shown going into the cafeteria) with the sound off.

■ After viewing, have students work in pairs or small groups to discuss the questions.

■ Tell students they will find out the answers when they watch the video.

Optional activity

Pair work Books closed. With the sound off, play the opening scene of Lynn in her office. Stop, and fast forward to the Hawaiian scene at the end of the sequence. Have students, working in pairs, speculate about what happens to Lynn between the office scene and the Hawaiian scene. If necessary, prompt students with questions such as "Do you think Lynn quit her job?" "Do you think she's on vacation?" Have students build a story and then watch the entire sequence, with the sound off, to check their predictions. (10–15 minutes)

 Watch the video

4 GET THE PICTURE

In this activity, students watch and listen to the sequence to find the answers to basic questions about Lynn's job and her career goals.

■ Books open. Explain the activity, and lead students through the questions and the possible answers. (If you wish, encourage students to answer if they feel they already have enough information.)

■ Tell students to check the correct answer for each question as they watch and listen to the video sequence.

■ Play the entire sequence with the sound on. Then have students compare answers with a partner.

■ Ask if anyone needs to see the sequence again to finish the task. Replay as needed.

■ Check answers, and encourage students to supply reasons for their choices.

Answers

1) She's a manager.
2) She works long hours.
3) Work in a hotel.

Optional activity

Books open. Show the sequence again, and ask students to call out "Stop" when they see or hear information that answers a question. Continue until each of the three questions has been covered. (5 minutes)

5 WATCH FOR DETAILS

In this activity, students focus more closely on details in order to decide whether statements about the story are true or false.

■ Books open. Explain the task, and read through the list of statements. Answer any questions about vocabulary or content.

■ Have students predict whether each statement is true or false and then compare their predictions with other students.

■ Play the sequence with the sound on. Have students check their predictions, marking each statement as true or false as they watch.

■ Replay the sequence as necessary, and then have students compare answers with a partner. Check answers around the class.

■ Have students work individually or in pairs to correct the false statements. If necessary, replay the sequence, and then check answers around the class.

Answers
1) False (Lynn works at AdTech.)
2) True
3) True
4) False (She works six days a week.)
5) False (She's studying hotel management.)
6) False (Bob's friend works in Hawaii.)
7) True

Optional activity

Pair work Books closed. Ask each pair to write five statements about the sequence: two true and three false. Have pairs exchange statements and then watch the sequence again to mark each statement as true or false. To complete the task, have students correct the false statements.
(10 minutes)

Possible answers
True statements
Lynn works ten hours a day.
Lynn wants to work in a hotel.

False statements
Lynn and Bob know each other. (Corrected: Lynn and Bob don't know each other.)
Lynn is taking classes on the weekends. (Corrected: Lynn is taking classes in the evening.)
Bob is a hotel worker. (Corrected: Bob is a lawyer.)

6 GIVING REASONS

In this activity, students give reasons for why they think Lynn doesn't like her work at AdTech and for why she wants to work in a hotel.

■ Books open. Read through the instructions with the class, and go over the pictures and captions.

■ *Pair work* Have students work in pairs to complete the chart.

■ Check answers around the class, and encourage students to provide evidence from the video to justify their choices. Replay the sequence as needed.

Possible answers
Reasons why Lynn doesn't like AdTech
She works on weekends.
There's too much telephone and computer work.
She wants to do something new.
The company is in a cold climate.
(The other reasons listed also could be placed under this column in the chart.)

Reasons why Lynn wants to work in a hotel
She's interested in hotel management.
She likes to travel.
She wants to do something new.

(see next page for optional activities)

Optional activities

A *Group work* Books open. Have students think of two additional reasons to add to each column. (5 minutes)

Possible answers

Reasons why Lynn doesn't like AdTech
She's tired.
She doesn't like working alone.

Reasons why Lynn wants to work in a hotel
She wants to meet new people.
She wants to live in an exciting place.

B *Pair work* Books closed. Ask students if they think Lynn would be happy in Hawaii. Have students work in pairs to list the advantages and disadvantages of working at a hotel there. (10 minutes)

Possible answers

Possible advantages
warm weather; beautiful beaches; relaxing; interesting people

Possible disadvantages
far from home; expensive place to live; have to work long hours

Follow-up

7 ROLE PLAY *Jobs*

In these communicative activities, students have the chance to be creative by taking the roles of employees at AdTech and talking about their work there.

Set the scene for the role plays by explaining that AdTech is a big company, and once a year there's an office party so people can get to know each other. Tell students that they will be taking the roles of AdTech employees at this party.

A Books open. Describe the task, and tell students to take turns playing B, an employee in another department of AdTech. (If you wish, take the role of B, and model the task with a student.)

■ *Pair work* Have students role-play, and then ask pairs to share their conversations with the class.

B Books open. Go over the instructions, and remind students to begin by introducing themselves to each other.

■ *Group work* Have students talk in groups of four. Mix with the groups, and encourage students to expand on what they like and dislike about their jobs.

■ Follow up by discussing as a class which students have the most interesting jobs and why.

Language close-up

8 *WHAT DID THEY SAY?*

This cloze activity develops bottom-up listening skills by having students complete the first part of the conversation among Paula, Lynn, and Bob.

■ Have students, working individually or in pairs, read the conversation and fill in any blanks they can before watching the sequence.

■ Play this segment of the video (with the picture off if you prefer) as many times as necessary while students work alone to check their predictions and complete the task. Then have students work in pairs to compare answers.

■ Go over answers with the class, and then replay the segment as students follow along in their books.

■ Model the conversation or, if you wish, do choral or individual repetition to prepare for group work. Then have students practice the conversation in groups of three.

Answers
Paula: Hi, Lynn! How are **you** doing?
Lynn: Oh, **hi**, Paula. Pretty **good**, thanks. How are you?
Paula: Not **bad**. Say, you **know** Bob Wallace, don't you?
Lynn: Oh, no, I don't **think** so. Hi, **I'm** Lynn Parker.
Bob: Pleased to **meet** you.
Paula: So, **how's** everything?
Lynn: **Do** you really **want** to know?
Paula: Of course **I** do.

Optional activities

A Books open. Ask students why Lynn says "Do you really want to know?" in response to Paula's asking her "So, how's everything?" Explain that asking someone how he or she is, is a greeting that usually requires only a simple response such as, "Fine, thanks." In this case, Lynn wants to make sure it is OK to tell Paula about her unhappiness at work. (5 minutes)

B *Group work* Books open. Have students work in groups of three to role-play a similar conversation using information of their own. (5 minutes)

9 *WH-QUESTIONS WITH DO; PREPOSITIONS*

To reinforce the important structures featured in this sequence, students practice asking Wh-questions with *do* and using the correct prepositions when answering.

A Books open. Explain the task, and go over the examples.

■ Have students work alone to fill in the blanks in the conversations and then compare their answers with a partner.

■ Check answers, and review the structures as needed.

■ Have students practice the conversations in pairs.

Answers
1) Bob: Where do you work, Lynn?
   Lynn: I work at AdTech. It's a computer software company.
   Bob: What do you do there?
   Lynn: I'm a manager in customer service.

2) Bob: Where do you go to school, Lynn?
   Lynn: I go to Franklin University. I'm studying hotel management.

3) Lynn: What do you do, Bob?
   Bob: I'm a lawyer.
   Lynn: Oh. Where do you work?
   Bob: I work at the law firm of Christopher Brown.

B *Pair work* Books open or closed. Have students practice similar conversations using information of their own or information they make up.

10 *ASKING ABOUT JOBS*

In this activity, students practice asking and
answering questions about work.

▪ Books open. Explain the task, and go over the
example. Encourage students to try to think of
some Wh-questions with *do*.

▪ *Pair work* Have students work in pairs to
think of appropriate questions. Then have
students change partners and ask and answer
the questions.

▪ Check questions and answers around the class,
and review as necessary.

Possible answers
1) What hotel do you work at?
2) What are your hours?
3) What do you do exactly?
4) Where are the tourists from?

Optional activity

Pair work Books open or closed. Have students
work in pairs to role-play a telephone
conversation between Lynn and Bob's friend who
works at a hotel in Hawaii, in which she asks him
about his job and about life there. (10 minutes)

Possible conversations

Lynn:	How do you like your work?
Bob's friend:	I love it, but the hours are long.
Lynn:	Oh, really? What about the weekends? What do you do then?
Bob's friend:	Well, I work on Saturdays also.
Lynn:	How do you like Hawaii?
Bob's friend:	It's wonderful! The weather is great, and the people are very friendly.
Lynn:	What do you do in your free time?
Bob's friend:	I go to the beach . . .

Jobs

Preview

1 *VOCABULARY* Jobs

In this activity, students work with the names of some of the various occupations presented in the documentary by matching job titles with pictures of people at work.

■ Books open. Explain the task. Then model the vocabulary for students, and have them examine the pictures.

■ *Pair work* Have students work together in pairs to complete the task. Then have pairs join together to form small groups and compare their answers.

■ Go over the answers with the class.

Answers
1) lawyer	4) cashier	7) chef
2) architect	5) bank teller	8) photographer
3) pianist	6) doctor	9) travel agent

2 GUESS THE FACTS

In this activity, students prepare to watch the documentary by predicting which of the jobs presented in the video are done by men and which are done by women.

■ Books open. Explain the task, and ask students to review the pictures in Exercise 1.

■ Point to the picture of the lawyer. Say, "Do you think the lawyer in the video is a man or a woman? Make a guess. Mark an *M* for man or a *W* for woman. Now do the same for the other eight jobs."

■ *Pair work* Have students work in pairs to complete the task and then compare their predictions with a new partner or in small groups.

■ Have several students share their predictions with the class. Do not give the answers at this point. Tell students that they will check their predictions in the next exercise.

Optional activities

A Books open. Ask students the following questions: "Which of these jobs are usually done by men in your culture? Which are usually done by women?"

■ Have students do the exercise again, but this time base their answers on information that is true for their cultures.

■ Have students compare answers with a partner or in small groups. (5 minutes)

B Books open. On the board, write the following information in chart format:

Job   Interesting: Yes   No

■ Have students work alone to complete the chart based on the occupations listed in Exercise 1. Then have them compare their charts in small groups.

■ Bring the class back together, and have students share their opinions by raising their hands to indicate that they think a job is interesting. (10 minutes)

Watch the video

3 GET THE PICTURE

In this activity, students watch and listen in order to write the occupations of some of the people presented in the documentary under their photos in the Video Activity Book.

■ Books open. Explain the task. Then play the entire sequence once or twice, and have students write each person's occupation under his or her photo.

■ Have students compare their answers with a partner or around the class. Play the documentary again, and have students check their answers. Then review the answers with the class.

(procedure continues on next page)

Answers

1) reporter
2) architect
3) lawyer
4) pianist
5) computer engineer
6) cashier
7) bank teller
8) doctor

Optional activity

Books open or closed. Have students watch the documentary again in order to say one additional thing about each person or their job (e.g., "The bank teller counts money." "The cashier works inside."). (5 minutes)

4 WATCH FOR DETAILS

In this activity, students watch and listen in order to answer more detailed questions about Rick Armstrong and Sylvia Davis.

■ Books open. Explain the task, and lead the class through the information in the box.

■ Play this segment of the documentary once or twice, and have students work alone to answer the questions about the two people.

■ Have students compare their answers with a partner or in small groups.

■ Play this section of the documentary again, and have students check their answers. Then review the answers with the class.

Possible answers

Rick Armstrong
1) commercial photographer
2) enjoys meeting people/job is exciting/
   something different every day
3) he takes many pictures of the same thing

Sylvia Davis
1) travel agent/owns a travel agency
2) she loves to travel/job is interesting/
   job is always different
3) there's a lot of phone work/
   she writes a lot of faxes/she's very busy/
   owning a business is a lot of responsibility

 *Follow-up*

5 ROLE PLAY *Interview*

In this extension activity, students build on what they have learned about various occupations in the documentary by taking turns playing the role of a reporter and interviewing classmates about jobs they have chosen.

■ Books open. Explain the task, and model the sample conversation.

■ Have each student choose one of the occupations presented in the video to role-play. As an option, have them complete the chart from Exercise 4 with information about the job they have chosen. Encourage students to be creative.

■ *Class activity* Have students stand and move around the room, asking at least three people about their jobs.

■ Bring the class back together, and ask several students to describe their jobs.

Optional activity

Pair work Books open or closed. Have students take turns playing the role of either Sylvia Davis or Rick Armstrong, as their partner interviews them about his or her job. (5 minutes)

3 At a garage sale

Topics/functions: Buying and selling
things; expressing opinions

Structures: *How much* and *how old*

Summary

The sequence takes place at a suburban garage
sale, where Fred and Susan have stopped and are
looking at various items for sale. Fred finds an old
camera, but Susan doesn't think he really wants
it. Susan sees a necklace and a bracelet she likes,
but Fred, worried that the price might be high,
says they are just OK. Then Susan finds a lovely
old watch. When the woman tells her it is twenty-
five dollars, Fred is shocked, but Susan decides to
buy it and the necklace and bracelet. Suddenly,
the woman's husband realizes that the watch was
his mother's. He tells Susan the watch is not for
sale and leads his wife away to talk about her
mistake. Meanwhile, Fred finds a motorcycle for
sale. The scene ends with Susan, still
disappointed about the watch, telling Fred that
he doesn't need the motorcycle.

Preview

1 CULTURE

In the video, Fred and Susan are shoppers at a
garage sale. Garage or yard sales are very popular
in the United States and Canada. People have
garage or yard sales to get rid of things they no
longer want and to make extra money. Many
people go to these sales hoping to find everyday
items they like or need at reasonable prices.
Sometimes they can buy valuable items at low
prices. The culture preview in the Video Activity
Book introduces students to the concept of garage
and yard sales and includes two sample ads that
list common household items frequently found at
such sales.

■ Books closed. To introduce the concept of
garage sales, first tell students that you recently
bought *a book* at a *shopping mall*, and write the

name of the item and the place on the board. Ask
a few students to name items they have bought
recently and the places where they bought them.
List the items and places on the board, helping
with vocabulary as necessary.

■ Continue by asking students to name places
where they can buy things in addition to the ones
already listed (e.g., grocery store, department
store, drugstore), and list these on the board, too.
Then ask if anyone has ever bought something at
a garage sale. (Note: If students say they do not
know what a garage sale is, tell them that they
are going to read some information about them.)

■ To prepare students for reading the culture
information about garage sales, write the
following questions on the board, and read them
aloud (these questions are not given in the Video
Activity Book). For your reference, possible
answers are included in parentheses.

1) What things are sold at a garage sale?
   (furniture, jewelry, clothing)
2) Who decides on prices? (the people who have
   the garage sale)
3) How do people know that there is a garage
   sale? (there is a sign in front of the house)

■ Books open. Tell students, working individually,
to read the culture information and find the
answers to the questions listed on the board.

■ Ask selected students to share their answers,
and check answers around the class.

■ Next have students read through the two ads
and circle the names of items for sale. Then ask
students to call out the names of the items as you
list them on the board.

Answers

Garage sale	*Yard sale*
children's clothes	antiques
kitchen items	books
TV	clock
	stereo
	bicycle

(procedure continues on next page)

- Put students into groups to answer the questions and name old items they have at home. Have each students choose one item to sell.

- Have each group share answers with the class.

---

2 VOCABULARY *Garage sale items*

This activity asks students to categorize common household items pictured in the book that could be sold at a garage sale and encourages them to think of additional items to categorize.

- Books open. Have students look at the pictures, and explain that these are items often sold at garage sales.

- *Pair work* Have students work in pairs to complete the chart and then compare answers with another pair.

- Check answers around the class. Ask students to call out the names of additional items they listed. Confirm answers by writing them on the board.

Answers

Kitchen items	*Jewelry*	*Other*
dishes	a bracelet	books
cups and saucers	a necklace	a camera
	a watch	a motorcycle

Additional items

Kitchen items	*Jewelry*	*Other*
bowls	earrings	a bicycle
forks	a ring	clothing
glasses		furniture
spoons		a stereo
		a TV

3 GUESS THE STORY

In these activities, students prepare to watch the sequence by making predictions about what the man and the woman buy based on visual information.

A Books open. Explain the task, making sure students understand that they should circle items in their charts on page 13. Then play the entire sequence with the sound off.

- Have students compare answers with a partner. Then check answers around the class, and replay the sequence again as necessary.

Answers

The following items should be circled in each student's chart. Students may also see other items in the video that they have listed in their charts (e.g., a bicycle).

Kitchen items	*Jewelry*	*Other*
dishes	a bracelet	a camera
	a necklace	a motorcycle
	a watch	

B Books open. Read the instructions, and tell students, working individually or in pairs, to refer to the items circled in their charts to complete this task. (If you wish, play the sequence with the sound off again before students make their predictions.)

- Have students compare lists with a partner. Then ask a few students to share their lists with the class, but do not give the answers at this point. Tell students that they will check their predictions in the next activity.

Watch the video

4 WHAT'S YOUR OPINION?

In this activity, students watch and listen to the entire sequence to decide what items they think Fred and Susan really do buy at the garage sale. (Note: In this sequence, neither Fred nor Susan is shown actually buying – that is, paying for – any of the items. However, students should be able to judge from the dialogue which items listed in the chart Fred and Susan will buy and which ones they will not buy.)

■ Books open. Explain the task, and read the list of items in the chart. Remind students that they need to watch and listen for information that will help them form opinions about what Fred and Susan buy.

■ Play the entire sequence with the sound on. Have students check *Yes* or *No* for each item as they watch and listen.

■ Check to see if anyone needs to watch the sequence again to finish the task, and replay as needed. Then have students compare answers with a partner.

■ Check answers, and encourage students to supply reasons to support their opinions. (Alternatively, you may wish to play the sequence again and have students call out "Stop" when information is presented that helped them form their opinions. Explain that you will stop the video to give them time to state their opinions aloud.)

Most likely opinions

1) the camera	*No*
2) the motorcycle	*No*
3) the necklace	*Yes*
4) the bracelet	*Yes*
5) the watch	*No*

5 MAKING INFERENCES

In this activity, students learn to make inferences, even when information is not explicitly stated, by watching and listening for information about Fred and Susan's opinions of the items at the garage sale.

■ Books open. Have students look at the four photos as you read each item. Then have students work in pairs to predict the answers.

■ Play the sequence with the sound on. Have students work alone to check their predictions, marking the best answers as they watch. Explain that sometimes the characters don't say "I like this" or "I don't like this," but it is still possible to guess their opinion. You may wish to tell students that this is called making inferences.

■ Check to see if anyone needs to view the sequence again, and replay as necessary. Then have students compare answers with a partner.

■ Check answers around the class, and encourage students to give reasons for their choices.

Answers
1) too old.
2) just all right.
3) too expensive.
4) Possible answer: The man tells his wife that his mother's watch is very important to him.

Optional activity

To expand on the activity in the Video Activity Book, follow this procedure.

■ Books open. Play the sequence, and stop the tape at the scene that contains the information needed to complete statement (a) (just after Susan asks Fred if he really needs the camera).

■ With the tape stopped, ask students to read the completed statement.

■ Then replay just that section of the sequence, in slow motion if possible, and have students list the visual and language clues that led them to choose their answer (e.g., Susan's facial expression, tone of voice, intonation pattern, and what she says imply that she thinks the camera is too old).

■ Follow this procedure with the other three items as well. (10 minutes)

Follow-up

Language close-up

6 GARAGE SALE

In these communicative activities, students practice buying and selling items as they role-play a class garage sale. The first activity prepares students for the role play by having them practice typical conversations between buyers and sellers. The second activity gives students the opportunity to buy and sell as if at a real garage sale.

A Pair work Books open. Say to students, "You are at a garage sale. Here are two conversations you might hear." Then explain the task.

■ Have students number the sentences and then check and practice the conversations with a partner.

Answers

1) 4 And how much are these earrings?
   1 Hello. Can I help you?
   3 It's twelve dollars.
   2 Yes, how much is this bracelet?
   5 They're twenty dollars.
   6 Thanks. I'll think about it.

2) 1 Can I help you?
   4 Oh, that's pretty expensive.
   6 OK. I'll take it.
   2 Yes, how much is this watch?
   5 Well, how about thirty dollars?
   3 It's forty dollars.

B Class activity Books open. Read the instructions above the chart, and then divide the class into two groups, A and B. Have each group complete the chart by listing six items to sell and assigning a price to each item.

■ Read the instructions below the chart, and ask students if they have any questions. Set up the role play: Group A, the sellers, display their charts on desks or tables, and Group B, the buyers, browse, looking for things they want to buy. Remind students that they can negotiate prices as in conversation (b) in part 1 of the activity. (Note: It is a good idea to set a time limit of 5–10 minutes.)

■ Have the groups change roles and repeat the process of buying and selling.

7 WHAT DID THEY SAY?

This cloze activity develops bottom-up listening skills by having students complete the first part of the conversation between Fred and Susan.

■ Books open. Have students, working individually or in pairs, read the conversation and fill in any blanks they can before watching the sequence.

■ Play this segment of the video (with the picture off if you prefer) as many times as necessary while students work alone to check their predictions and complete the task. Then have students compare answers with a partner.

■ Go over answers with the class. Then replay the segment as students follow along in their books and check their work.

■ Model the conversation or, if you wish, lead a choral or individual repetition of it. Then have students practice the conversation in pairs.

Answers

Fred: Hey, Susan, how do you **like** this?
Susan: Oh, **please**, Fred.
Fred: Oh, come on. It's only a **dollar**!
Susan: **Do** you really **want** it, Fred?
Fred: No, I guess **you're** right.
Vendor: Can I **help** you?
Fred: No, thanks **anyway**. We're just **looking**.
Susan: Oh, Fred, **come** over here. Just look at this lovely, old **necklace**!
Fred: Yeah, it's **OK**.
Susan: It's **not** just OK, Fred. It's very **nice**!

Optional activities

A Group work Books open. Working in groups of three, have students act out the scene, imitating the actors in the sequence as closely as they can. Encourage students to take turns playing each role. (10 minutes)

B Pair work Books open. Have students rewrite the conversation so that Susan is really excited about the camera and Fred thinks the necklace is a wonderful discovery. (15 minutes)

8 *EXPRESSING OPINIONS*

In this activity, students focus their attention on the language Fred uses to express his opinions.

- Books open. Explain the task, and read each item. Have students work alone to predict answers and then compare their choices with a partner.

- Play the entire sequence with the sound on. Remind students to listen carefully to what Fred says to check their predictions. Then ask selected students to describe what is happening in the sequence when Fred says each of these things. [For (1) and (2), Fred is showing Susan the camera; for (3), Susan is showing him the necklace; for (4), the vendor tells Susan that the bracelet and necklace are $15; for (5), the vendor says the watch is $25.]

- Replay the sequence, and have students complete the task by checking the correct answers.

- Have students compare answers with a partner, and encourage them to explain the reasons for their choices.

- Go over answers with the class, and replay the sequence as needed.

Answers
1) What do you think of this?
2) Please let me [buy it].
3) I like it a little.
4) The price is reasonable.
5) I don't believe it!

Optional activity

Books closed. Have students watch the sequence again and make a list of things that Fred and Susan do or say to show that they do not really like something. (10 minutes)

Possible answers
Susan to Fred
About the camera: "Oh, please, Fred!"
About the motorcycle: Susan puts her hands on her hips, shakes her head, and says, "Oh, no, Fred! Not the motorcycle!"

Fred to Susan
About the necklace: "Yeah, it's OK." (in a negative tone of voice)
About the watch: "Susan, are you kidding? Twenty-five dollars for that old watch!" Later, when Susan says she'll take the watch, Fred throws his hands in the air, and says "OK" in disgust.

9 HOW MUCH *AND* HOW OLD

In this activity, students complete questions with *how much* or *how old* and the correct form of the verb *be*, the grammatical focus of the sequence.

A Books open. Explain the task, and go over the example. Provide additional examples of the structures if necessary.

- Have students work alone to complete the questions and then compare answers with a partner.

- Check answers around the class, and review as necessary.

Answers
1) How much is this necklace?
   How old is it?
2) How much are these books?
   And how old are they?
3) How old are these shoes?
   How much are they?

B *Pair work* Books open. Have students practice the conversations, replacing the items given with items of their own.

Optional activity

Pair work Books open. Have students develop similar conversations with various items, prices, and ages of items. (10 minutes)

4 What kind of movies do you like?

Topics/functions: Expressing likes and dislikes; making plans

Structures: Object pronouns

Summary

The sequence opens with Alfredo, Bill, and Pat coming out of a restaurant where they have just had dinner. They wander down the street and then stop to discuss their plan for the rest of the evening. They decide to rent a movie on video and walk to a neighborhood video store. Once there, however, they can't agree on a movie to watch. Finally, Alfredo suggests going to listen to some music since he knows a terrific group that's playing at a nearby cafe. Bill and Pat agree, assuming it's a rock band. But soon they discover that Alfredo is talking about a country and western group, and Bill doesn't like country and western music. Pat suggests a jazz concert, but Bill doesn't like jazz either. The sequence closes with the three wandering down the street again, still without plans for the evening.

 **Preview**

1 CULTURE

In this sequence, Alfredo, Bill, and Pat go to their neighborhood video shop to look for a movie to rent. The culture preview in the Video Activity Book gives students some background information on the rising number of video rental stores in the United States and Canada.

■ Books closed. To introduce the topic, ask the class the following questions, and have them respond by raising their hands to indicate "yes" (these questions are not given in the Video Activity Book).
1) Do you like movies?
2) Do you watch videos at home?
3) Is there a video store in your neighborhood?

■ Books open. Lead students through the information in the culture preview. Answer vocabulary and content questions as needed.

■ Read the three questions, and have students work in pairs to answer them.

■ Check answers around the class.

Optional activity

■ *Group work* Books closed. Have students make a group list of favorite movies by asking each other, "What's your favorite movie?" and listing the responses.

■ Have the groups report orally to the class. Create a class list by writing the favorite movie titles on the board as the groups read them. (10 minutes)

2 VOCABULARY *Kinds of movies*

This activity introduces the names of various genres, or types, of movies, including those presented in the video, and gives students a chance to express their opinions about them.

■ Books open. Lead students through the list of movie types in the chart, using the corresponding photos to point out examples. Note that the movie *Dracula* is categorized as a "classic," but it could also be considered a horror film. You may wish to give additional movie titles that students are likely to know.

■ Lead students through the four opinion statements listed at the top of the chart by reading each one expressively to help convey its meaning.

■ Explain the task by giving your opinion of the first two or three movie types. Then have students complete the chart on their own before sharing responses in groups or around the class.

Optional activities

A *Group work* Books open. Have students work together to decide on the group's favorite and least favorite movie types. Then have each group report to the class while you list the results on the board. (5 minutes)

B *Group work* Books closed. Have students work together to brainstorm additional movie and/or videos types. Then have each group report to the class. (5 minutes)

Possible answers

musicals, documentaries, concert films, dance movies, biographies, sports stories, nature films, children's movies, music videos

3 GUESS THE STORY

In this activity, students prepare to watch the sequence by making predictions about the story based on visual information.

■ Books open. Ask students, working in pairs, to look at the three photos and guess the answer to the question under each one.

■ Have selected students report their predictions to the class. Accept all answers at this point.

■ Tell students they will watch the beginning of the video sequence without the sound and they should check their predictions against what they see.

■ Play the first two minutes of the sequence with the sound off as students watch and check their predictions.

■ Ask students, working in pairs or small groups, to answer the three questions again. Check answers around the class, accepting all reasonable answers. Explain to students that any doubts will be cleared up as they continue watching the sequence.

 Watch the video

4 GET THE PICTURE

In this activity, students watch and listen to decide whether four general statements about the video sequence are true or false.

■ Books open. Explain the task, and lead students through the four statements in the box. Remind students that they should concentrate on watching and listening for the information to complete the task.

■ Play the sequence with the sound on. Tell students to complete the task while watching and then compare answers with a partner.

■ Check answers around the class, and show the sequence again if necessary.

Answers

1) True   3) True
2) False   4) False

Optional activity

■ *Pair work* Books closed. Have students watch the sequence again and then work with a partner to write three statements about the sequence: two true and one false [e.g., "Pat likes science-fiction movies." (True) "Nobody likes country and western music." (False)].

■ Have pairs exchange statements and then watch the sequence again to mark each statement as true or false. To complete the task, have students correct the false statements. (10–15 minutes)

5 MAKING INFERENCES

In this activity, students learn to make inferences, even when information is not explicitly stated, by watching and listening for information about the kinds of movies and music Pat, Bill, and Alfredo like.

■ Books open. Explain the task, and then have students, working individually, complete any items they can before watching the sequence.

■ Play the entire sequence with the sound on. Tell students to complete the task as they watch and then compare answers with a partner. Explain that sometimes the characters don't say "yes" or "no" when asked if they like something, but it is still possible to guess the meaning. You may wish to tell students that this is called making inferences.

■ Check answers around the class, and play the sequence again as needed. [Note: Items that are very difficult are blacked out in the Video Activity Book, but in some cases the answers can be inferred (e.g., "Pat doesn't like suspense thrillers." "Alfredo doesn't like science-fiction movies.").]

Answers

	Pat	Bill	Alfredo
Movies			
science fiction	Y	N	–
suspense thrillers	–	Y	–
classic films	–	–	Y
horror films	Y	–	Y
westerns	–	N	–
Music			
country and western	–	N	Y
jazz	–	N	–

Optional activity

■ *Group work* Books closed. Divide the class into three equal teams: the Pat team, the Bill team, and the Alfredo team. Explain that the members of each team should listen carefully to everything their character says and write down exactly what he says to show his likes and dislikes. Tell students that while they are watching the sequence, they can call out "Stop," and you will stop the video to rewind it or to give them time to write.

■ Play the sequence until someone asks you to stop. Proceed in this manner until most students are satisfied.

■ Have team members compare what they have written, and write a team master list on the board.

■ Go over each team's master list, and explain and review as appropriate. (20 minutes)

Possible answers

Pat: Now here are some great science-fiction films!

Bill: Well, gee. I really don't like country and western very much!

Alfredo: I really like classic films a lot!

6 WHAT'S THE PROBLEM?

In this activity, students make inferences and relate their own experiences to the events in the sequence.

■ Books open. Read through the questions with students.

■ *Pair work* Put students in pairs to discuss the questions, and encourage them to give reasons for their answers. You may want to have one member of each pair record answers.

■ Have the pairs report their answers to the class.

Follow-up

7 FINISH THE STORY

In this activity, students use what they know about the characters to finish the story in a way they think makes sense.

■ Books open. Explain the task, and tell students to look at the sequence of photos.

■ *Group work* Put students in small groups to finish the story. Ask one person in each group to take notes. Set a time limit of 5–10 minutes.

■ At the end of the allotted time, have each group tell their ending of the story to the class.

8 MAKING PLANS

In this activity, students use the language presented in the sequence to make their own plans for an evening.

■ Books open. Explain the task, and have students look at the four advertisements of possible activities for the evening.

■ *Group work* Lead students through the example expressions. Then have students work in small groups to make plans for the evening.

■ Have groups report their plans for the evening to the class.

Optional activities

A *Group work* Books open. Tell students that they are going to work together again in small groups to make plans for the evening, using the ads in their books. Before the groups begin, prepare small slips of paper to distribute to each member in a group. Leave all the slips for a group blank, except one. On this slip, write the name Bill (the person from the video who didn't like any of the suggestions).

■ Distribute a slip to each group member, explaining that only one of the slips is labeled and that each person should keep his or her slip secret. Then explain that the student with the slip labeled Bill should not agree to any of the suggestions made and the others should try to find out who this person is and persuade him to accept one of the plans for the evening. (10 minutes)

B *Group work* Books closed. Bring in ads for upcoming events in your area, and have students work with them to make plans for the weekend. If you wish, follow the same procedure described in the preceding activity. (15 minutes)

 Language close-up

9 WHAT DID THEY SAY?

This cloze activity has students complete the first part of the conversation among Bill, Alfredo, and Pat.

■ Books open. Have students, working individually or in pairs, read the conversation and fill in any blanks they can before watching the sequence.

■ Play this segment of the video as students work alone to check their predictions and complete the task.

■ Have students compare answers with a partner, make further predictions, and then watch the segment again.

■ Repeat the preceding step as many times as needed, and then go over the answers with the class.

■ Model the conversation or, if you wish, do choral or individual repetition to prepare for group work. Then have students practice the conversation in groups of three.

Answers
Bill: So, . . . what **do** we **do** now?
Alfredo: What **time** is it?
Bill: **Seven** o'clock.
Pat: Look, **we** all like **movies**. Why don't we **rent** a video and **watch** it at my **house**?
Bill: That's **not** a bad **idea**, Pat.
Alfredo: It's **OK** with **me**.
Pat: Well, then, **come** on! . . .
    Now here **are** some great **science-**fiction movies! **What** do you **think**, Bill?
Bill: Uh, I can't **stand** sci-fi. How **about** a good **suspense** thriller?
Pat: Uh . . . Alfredo, **what** about you? **What** do you **think** of science **fiction**?
Alfredo: Oh, it's **OK**.

Optional activity

Group work Books open. Have students form groups of three and rework the dialogue so that all three friends like science fiction and decide to rent a sci-fi movie. (5 minutes)

10 *OBJECT PRONOUNS*

In this activity, students work with object pronouns to ask and answer questions about movies.

A Books open. Explain the task, and go over the example given.

■ Have students, working individually, fill in the correct object pronouns and then compare answers with a partner.

■ Check answers around the class.

Answers

1) them   4) him
2) her   5) them
3) it   6) it

B *Pair work* Books open. Have students take turns asking and answering the questions, giving their own opinions. Then have several pairs each share a question-and-answer set with the class.

11 *EXPRESSING LIKES AND DISLIKES*

In this activity, students practice giving and responding to opinions about movies, actors, and actresses.

■ Books open. Explain the task. Then lead students through the short conversations, giving them a chance to practice the responses chorally and individually.

■ *Pair work* Have students take turns giving opinions and responding.

Optional activity

■ *Pair work* Books open. Have students work with a partner to write five statements similar to those given in their books.

■ Have students change partners and take turns giving and responding to opinions.

■ Have several pairs share their best statements and responses with the class. (10 minutes)

What's your favorite kind of music?

 **Preview**

1 VOCABULARY Kinds of music

In this class activity, students prepare to work with the theme of the documentary and the language in it by listing all the various kinds of music they can think of.

- Books open. Explain the task, and then have students work in groups of four or five to list as many kinds of music as they can think of.

- Bring the class back together, and have groups take turns calling out the names of types of music while you create a class list on the board.

 Watch the video

2 GET THE PICTURE

In this activity, students watch and listen to the documentary to find out what kinds of music are mentioned.

- Books open. Explain the task. Then play the entire documentary. Have students work alone to check off the music types they hear mentioned as they watch.

- Have students compare their answers with a partner. Then replay the documentary if there seems to be any doubt about the correct answers.

- Go over answers with the class either by having students call out the music types mentioned or by replaying the documentary and having students call out "Stop!" each time they hear one of the music types talked about.

Answers
All of the music types should be checked off *except* for folk and pop. (Note: In the sequence, both *blues* and *rhythm and blues* are mentioned. You may wish to tell students that a blues musician uses an acoustic guitar, while a musician performing rhythm and blues uses an electric guitar.)

Optional activity

Books open. Play the sequence again, and have students work alone to list the other types of music mentioned. Then have students compare answers with a partner. (5 minutes)

Answers
blues, Top 40, western swing, dancing music

3 WATCH FOR DETAILS

These activities ask students to focus more closely on details in the documentary by first having them watch and listen for the musical likes and dislikes of the people interviewed and then indicating which people play a musical instrument.

A Books open. Explain the task, and have students look carefully at the photos of the seven people from the documentary.

- Play the sequence, and have students check off the kinds of music each person likes as they watch.

- Have students compare answers with a partner or in small groups.

- Ask if anyone needs to watch the documentary again, and replay as necessary.

- Go over the answers with the class.

Answers

	1	2	3	4	5	6
country and western	✓	✓				
jazz			✓	✓	✓	
rock				✓		✓
classical					✓	
new wave				✓		

(procedure continues on next page)

31

B Books open. Explain the task. Then play the sequence, and have students work alone to write the name of the musical instrument each person plays.

▪ Have students compare their answers with a partner, and then go over them with the class.

Answers
1) doesn't play an instrument
2) guitar
3) saxophone
4) piano
5) guitar

Optional activities

A Books open. Have students look at the photos in the second part of Exercise 3 again. Replay the documentary, and have students write the kind(s) of music that the people pictured dislike. Tell students that two people don't say.

▪ Have students compare answers with a partner, and then go over them with the class. (5 minutes)

Answers
1) Top 40
2) doesn't say
3) country western
4) country western, rock
5) doesn't say

B Books open. Replay the documentary, and have students watch and listen to find out how often each person interviewed goes to a music club.

▪ Have students check their answers with a partner, and then go over them with the class. (5 minutes)

Answers
1) twice a week
2) a couple of times a month
3) once a month
4) pretty often
5) once a week

4 THE REPORTER'S QUESTIONS

In this activity, students focus on detail by watching and listening in order to identify all the questions that the reporter asks.

▪ Books open. Explain the task, and read through the list of questions with the class.

▪ Play the entire sequence. Have students check off the questions they hear as they watch and then compare answers with a partner.

▪ Replay the documentary if needed before going over the answers with the class. (Note: You may want to go over the answers by playing the documentary again and having students call out, "Stop!" each time they hear one of the reporter's questions. Stop the video when asked to, and then select a student to call out the question asked. Proceed through the documentary in this manner until all of the questions have been covered.)

Answers
How often do you (get to) go to nightclubs?
What's your favorite kind of music?
How often do you listen to live music?
What's your least favorite kind of music?
Do you play a musical instrument (yourself)?
What do you think of country and western music?

Optional activity

▪ *Pair work* Books open. Play the documentary again, and have pairs list any other questions the reporter asks. If possible, give the video control to one of the students, and allow this student to stop and restart the video as the rest of the class writes out the questions they hear.

▪ Have pairs form small groups to compare answers, and then replay the video to check. (10 minutes)

Answers
What kind of music do they play here?
How do you like this music?

5 CLASS INTERVIEW

In these activities, students use the information they have learned to conduct interviews with classmates about their musical likes and dislikes.

A Books open. Explain the task, and model the sample conversation.

■ *Class activity* Have everyone stand and move around the room, interviewing at least three classmates.

B Bring the class back together, and compile a class list of favorite and least favorite musical types on the board.

Optional activities

A *Group work* Books open or closed. Have students work in small groups to talk about what they like and dislike about each of the clubs shown in the documentary. (5 minutes)

B *Group work* Books open or closed. Play short pieces of different types of music, including some that are currently popular in your area. Have students form small groups to talk about what they like and dislike about each kind of music. (10 minutes)

5 A family picnic

Topics/functions: Talking about family

Structures: Present continuous and simple present

Summary

In the opening scenes of the sequence, Freddy Hernandez arrives at a park with his wife Linda and young daughter Angela. His mother, father, sister, aunt, uncle, and cousins are already there, setting up for a family picnic. Freddy's brother Rick arrives with his friend Betsy Scott, and before they join the group, Rick points out some of his relatives and answers Betsy's questions about his family. When they join the group, Rick introduces Betsy to various family members. Rick's aunt Marta gathers everyone together for a family photo, and Betsy takes a picture of the group.

Preview

1 CULTURE

In the video, the Hernandez family is having a family picnic, although relatives who live in Mexico are not present. The culture preview introduces the topic of families and family gatherings by providing data on families and moving patterns in the United States and Canada.

■ Books closed. To introduce the topic of families, write the following sentences on the board:
1) In the U.S. and Canada, _____ percent of all people say family is the most important part of life.
2) Children often leave home at age _____ .
3) _____ percent of all families move every year.

■ Lead students through the sentences and ask, "What numbers do you think go in the blanks?" Have students, working individually, guess and then compare predictions with a partner.

■ Books open. Have students read the culture preview to check their predictions.

■ Go over the information presented, and answer vocabulary or content questions. Then read the questions with students, and have them answer in small groups.

■ Check answers around the class.

2 VOCABULARY Family

In this activity, students become familiar with vocabulary used in the sequence by labeling relatives in a family tree.

■ Books closed. To introduce this activity, ask students to call out the missing words in the following word pairs:

grandmother and _____ (grandfather)
sister and _____ (brother)
father and _____ (mother)
aunt and _____ (uncle)
nephew and _____ (niece)

Work with these in random order until students feel comfortable with the vocabulary.

■ *Pair work* Books open. Explain the task, and ask students to find Jane in the family tree.

■ Have students complete the task and then compare answers with another pair.

■ Check answers around the class, and review vocabulary as needed.

Answers
grandmother, grandfather
aunt, uncle; mother, father
brother, sister-in-law; JANE, husband;
    sister, brother-in-law
niece; daughter, son; nephew

Optional activity

- Books open. Have students make a quiz based on the family tree. Write an example question such as "What do you call your mother's son?" on the board, and ask students to answer (they should respond with the word "brother"). Then say to students, "Now I want you to write five more questions like this one."

- **Group work** Put students into groups of four or five to write questions. Circulate among the groups to help with accuracy.

- Have the groups quiz each other, and then have each group share its most difficult question with the class. (15 minutes)

Possible questions and answers
What do you call your aunt's husband? Uncle.
What do you call your brother's wife?
    Sister-in-law.
What do you call your mother's father?
    Grandfather.

3 GUESS THE STORY

In this activity, students use words from the vocabulary preview to make predictions about who they will see at the family picnic in the video sequence.

- Books open. Ask students to look at the photo of the Hernandez family. Hold your book up, point to someone in the picture, and say, for example, "Who is this? Is she the mother?" Have students call out guesses. Accept all answers at this point.

- Play the first minute of the sequence with the sound off (until Rick and Betsy are shown getting out of the car and walking toward the picnic area). Have students work alone and write their predictions as they watch.

- Have students compare their predictions with each other. Explain that they will find out the answers in the next activity.

Optional activity

- Books closed. Tell students they are going to watch the first part of the video with the sound off. They should list observations about the day, the place, the time of year, and the event (e.g., It's afternoon. They meet in a park. It's not crowded. It's summer. They're having a picnic.).

- Play the sequence with the sound off until the scene where Rick and Betsy join the rest of the family.

- Have students list observations and then compare them with a few classmates.

- Ask selected students to share their observations with the class. (10 minutes)

 Watch the video

4 GET THE PICTURE

In this activity, students watch and listen to find out which of Rick's relatives are at the picnic.

- Books open. Have students look again at the Hernandez family photo. Ask if they think Rick's parents are in it (yes, they are). Explain that since Rick's parents are at the picnic, *Yes* has been checked off in the chart. Tell students they will watch the video sequence to complete the rest of the chart.

- Play the entire sequence with the sound on. Have students complete the task while they watch.

- Check if anyone needs to watch the sequence again to finish the task, and replay as needed. Then have students compare answers with a partner.

Answers
1) Yes	5) No
2) Yes	6) Yes
3) Yes	7) No
4) Yes	8) Yes

Optional activity

Pair work Books open. Have students look at the photos of the Hernandez family in this unit and label as many family members as they can. (5 minutes)

5 WATCH FOR DETAILS

In this activity, students watch and listen for specific information needed to answer questions about Rick's family.

■ Books open. Explain the task, and read the questions with students, going over vocabulary as needed.

■ Books closed. Play the sequence with the sound on. Remind students to watch and listen for information that will help them answer the questions.

■ Books open. Have students, working individually or in pairs, answer the questions and then compare answers with a partner.

■ Check answers around the class. If there are errors, replay the sequence so that students can check their answers.

Answers
1) Mexico.
2) one brother and two sisters.
3) owns a business.
4) a boutique.
5) three years old.
6) night school.

6 WHAT'S YOUR OPINION?

In this activity, students discuss the ways in which Rick's family is the same as and is different from a typical family in the United States and Canada.

■ Books closed. Ask students to tell you what they know about Rick's family. Prompt with questions such as "Does Rick have a big family?" "Does Rick live near his parents?" "Where does Rick's older sister live?" "Where do his grandparents live?" "Do you think members of Rick's family see each other often?"

■ *Pair work* Books open. Explain the task, and have students read the culture preview on page 22 again. Encourage students to give reasons for their opinions as they discuss the question.

■ Have selected pairs share their ideas with the class.

Possible answer
Rick's family is like most families in the United States and Canada, but it is also different.
Similarities: Some people in his family live far away. Rick's sister and grandparents live in Mexico. The family is important to each other. They go on picnics together.
Differences: Rick lives near his parents. He probably sees his aunt a lot. She knows that he goes to night school.

Optional activity

■ *Group work* Books open or closed. Have students from the same cultural background work together in small groups to write three statements that are generally true about families in their culture.

■ Have groups share their statements with the class. (10 minutes)

7 YOUR FAMILY

These communicative activities deepen understanding by linking the content in this unit with students' backgrounds and experiences.

A Books open. Explain the task, and lead students through the questions.

■ *Pair work* Ask students to form pairs with a classmate they do not know well and to take turns asking questions about each other's families.

■ Ask selected students to tell the class about their partner's family.

B Books open. Explain the task, and give students up to 5 minutes to draw a picture of their family on a separate sheet of paper.

■ *Pair work* Have students take turns asking about each person in their partner's picture, using questions similar to those given as examples.

8 AN INTERESTING PERSON

In these communicative activities, students practice describing people.

A Books closed. To introduce this activity, tell the class briefly about an interesting relative or friend, and invite them to ask questions about this person.

■ Ask students to think of an interesting relative or friend they have.

■ *Pair work* Books open. Explain the task, and have students form pairs. Tell students that they may use the questions in the book to ask their partner about his or her relative or friend. If you would like, have students take notes about their partner's description to use in the next activity.

B Books open. Explain the task, and have students form pairs. Make sure students understand that they should talk about their partner's interesting relative or friend (from the first activity in this section).

■ As an optional step, you may ask selected students to tell the class about their own or their partner's friend or relative.

9 WHAT DID THEY SAY?

This cloze activity has students complete the first part of the conversation between Rick and Betsy.

■ Books open. Have students, working individually or in pairs, fill in any blanks they can before watching the sequence.

■ Play this segment of the video as many times as necessary while students check their predictions and complete the task.

■ Have students compare answers with a partner and then watch again to check their answers.

■ Have selected students read aloud lines of the conversation as you write the answers on the board.

■ Model the conversation or, if you wish, do choral or individual repetition to prepare for pair work. Then have pairs practice the conversation.

Answers
Betsy: So, how many **people** are there in your **family**, Rick?
Rick: A **lot**, if you count all my **cousins**.
Betsy: Do they all **live** here in the **States** now?
Rick: Oh, **no**. I have relatives in **Mexico**. My grandmother and **grandfather** are there, and my older **sister**, too.
Betsy: How many **sisters** do you have?
Rick: **Two**, plus an older **brother**. There's my **brother** Freddy over there with his **wife** Linda.
Betsy: Oh, really. What do they **do**?
Rick: Freddy **has** an import-export business, and Linda manages **a** boutique.
Betsy: Is that their **daughter**?
Rick: Yeah. Her **name**'s Angela.

Optional activity

Books open. Have students substitute their own information in the conversation, and then practice it with a partner. (5 minutes)

10 *PRESENT CONTINUOUS VS. SIMPLE PRESENT*
Asking about relatives

In these activities, students work with forms of *do* in the present continuous and simple present tenses to ask questions and make statements about family members.

A Books open. Explain the task. Have students complete the conversation and compare answers with a partner.

■ Check answers around the class, and review as needed. If you wish, have students practice the conversation in pairs.

Answers
A: Do all of your relatives live in the United States?
B: No, I **have** relatives in Mexico. My grandparents and older sister live there.
A: What does your sister do? Does she have a job?
B: No, she **isn't working** right now. She**'s going** to school.
A: Really? What is she studying?
B: She**'s studying** English literature. She **loves** it.
A: What about your grandparents? Are they still working or are they retired?
B: **They're (still) working**! And they're both 80 years old!

B Books open. Read the instructions and the sample question, asking students to provide examples of how it could be completed (e.g., "Do your parents live in your home country?"). Have students, working individually, write four more questions using the present continuous or simple present. Circulate to check for correct form.

Possible questions
Does your family see each other often?
Do you have any brothers or sisters?
Are they going to school now or are they working?

■ *Class activity* Have students circulate, asking one of their questions to a classmate and then moving on to ask another question to a different classmate. (If you wish, keep the activity moving by setting a maximum of 15 seconds for each

exchange – clapping your hands when the time is up.)

■ Follow up by having selected students ask you one of their questions.

Optional activities

A *Group work* Books open or closed. Have students, working in small groups, write three interesting questions to ask you about your family. Encourage students to be creative. At the same time, you might want to remind students that questions that are too personal are usually not polite. If you think it is necessary to emphasize this point, tell them to ask only those questions that they would enjoy answering as well.

■ Tell each group that they are allowed to ask you only their most interesting question, and then you will ask that same question to one of the students in another group. (10 minutes)

Possible questions
Do you look more like your mother or your father?
Is anyone else in your family studying English?
Do you have more than five brothers and sisters?

B *Group work* Books open or closed. Have students, working in small groups, write three to five questions to ask Betsy about her day with the Hernandez family.

■ Have one student from each group move to another group to play the role of Betsy. This student answers the group's questions. (Alternatively, play the role of Betsy yourself, and have each group ask you their two most interesting questions.) (10 minutes)

Possible questions and answers
Group: Do Rick and his brother look like each other?
Betsy: Yes, they really do!
Group: What does the Hernandez family like to eat?
Betsy: They like to eat Mexican and American food.
Group: What does Rick's aunt do?
Betsy: I don't know, but I don't think she's a photographer.

6 I like to stay in shape.

Topics/functions: Talking about routines
Structures: Adverbs of frequency

Summary

The sequence takes place in a park in the early morning, where Anne is jogging. Mark parks his car and then checks his hair in the mirror. He gets out and when Anne stops to rest, he approaches and greets her. From Anne's reaction, it is clear they do not know each other. She is polite, however, and Mark continues talking to her. Trying to impress her, he says that he gets up early, does aerobics, goes to a health club, jogs, and plays tennis and team sports. In reality, Mark does very few of these things. Each time he describes a sport or activity, a scene shows what he really does. Anne suspects that Mark is exaggerating, and she seems relieved when her friends arrive to jog with her. She invites Mark to join them. He looks embarrassed and says he doesn't have time. As Anne and her friends jog away, Mark approaches another person.

Preview

1 CULTURE

These days, most people in the United States and Canada know that regular exercise is very important, and a healthy lifestyle is highly valued. Still, 43 percent of people in the United States and Canada say they never or hardly ever exercise. The culture preview in the Video Activity Book prepares students to work with the unit by presenting them with information about sports and exercise in the United States and Canada.

■ Books closed. Ask students, "Do you exercise?" Have them respond by raising their hands to indicate "yes." Total the number of students who exercise. Then calculate the class percentage and write it on the board. Follow the same procedure with the question, "Do you play team sports?"

■ In more advanced classes, ask students, "Why do people exercise?" and have them work in pairs to list reasons. Write the various reasons on the board (e.g., to stay in shape, to lose weight, to build muscles, to have fun, to stay healthy).

■ Books open. Have students read the culture preview silently to compare class answers about exercise and sports with the information presented in the text.

■ Answer any content or vocabulary questions. Then have students work in pairs or small groups to answer the questions as you circulate around the class.

2 VOCABULARY Sports and exercise

These activities introduce the names of some sports and types of exercise, including those presented in this sequence.

A *Pair work* Books open. Explain the task, and ask students to look at the six illustrations. Then have students work in pairs to label the pictures.

■ Check answers around the class.

Answers
1) jogging	3) soccer	5) basketball
2) aerobics	4) swimming	6) volleyball

B Books open. Explain the task. If necessary, give an example of a team sport (baseball) and an individual activity (weight lifting).

■ Have students, working individually or in pairs, complete the chart. Encourage students to add additional words to the chart before comparing answers with classmates.

■ Check answers with the class, and then compile a class list of sports and activities on the board.

Answers
Individual activities	*Team sports*
jogging	basketball
aerobics	soccer
swimming	volleyball

(procedure continues on next page)

39

Additional sports and activities

Individual activities   *Team sports*

Rollerblading   baseball
ice-skating   hockey

Optional activities

A *Class activity* Books closed. Have students put the items in the class list of sports and activities into other categories (e.g., easy/difficult, expensive/cheap, equipment needed/no equipment needed). (5 minutes)

B *Group work* Books closed. Have students, working in small groups, take turns miming a sport or exercise type while the other group members guess what is being acted out. (5 minutes)

3 GUESS THE STORY

In this activity, students prepare to watch the sequence by making predictions, based on visual information, about who likes to exercise.

■ Books open. Have students look at the photo of Anne and Mark. Say, "This is Anne and Mark. Who do you think likes to exercise more?" Ask several students to guess. Accept all answers.

■ Books closed. Tell students to look at the video screen. Say, "Now, we're going to watch the beginning of the video without sound. After we watch, I'll ask you again about who you think likes to exercise more."

■ Play the first minute of the sequence with the sound off (until just after Mark is shown eating breakfast).

■ Ask students, "Who likes to exercise more, the man or the woman?" Students should be able to answer that the woman, Anne, does.

Optional activity

Pair work Books closed. Have students watch the beginning of the sequence again and then work in pairs to describe what Mark does before getting out of the car (e.g., "He looks in the mirror and fixes his hair."). (5 minutes)

 Watch the video

4 GET THE PICTURE

Here, students watch and listen to the entire sequence to determine whether the statements about Mark and/or Anne are true or false.

■ Books open. Explain the task, and lead students through the three statements. Have students predict whether each statement is true or false.

■ Play the sequence through with the sound on, and have students check the correct answers while watching. Then ask students to correct the false statements.

■ Have students compare answers with a partner.

■ Check if anyone needs to watch the sequence again to finish the task. Replay as needed, and check answers around the class.

Answers
1) False (Mark doesn't know Anne. They aren't friends.)
2) False (Mark doesn't like to exercise.)
3) True

Optional activities

A *Pair work* Books open or closed. Have students work in pairs to write three statements about the sequence – two true and one false [e.g., "Mark is good at tennis." (False)].

■ Have pairs exchange statements and then watch the sequence again to mark each statement as true or false. Then have students correct the false statements. (10 minutes)

B Books closed. Write the following statements on the board. Then have students watch the sequence again and look for visual clues that support the statements. For your reference, possible answers are given in parentheses.
1) Mark is not at the park to exercise. (He combs his hair; he's overweight; he's dressed too well.)
2) Mark doesn't know Anne. (He doesn't know her name; he tells her many things about himself.)
3) Anne is in better shape than Mark. (She enjoys jogging; she is not overweight.)

5 *WATCH FOR DETAILS*

In these activities, students focus more closely on details by watching and listening for the things Mark says he does versus the things he really does.

A Books open. Explain the task, and lead students through the nine illustrations. If you wish, have students predict answers before they watch the sequence.

■ Tell students, "Now, watch and listen for the things Mark *says* he does and check them in your books." Play the entire sequence with the sound on as students work alone to complete the task.

■ Have students compare answers with a partner. Then ask if anyone needs to watch the sequence again. Replay as necessary, and then check answers around the class.

Answers
Mark *says* that he does the following things:
He jogs to stay in shape.
He gets up early.
He does aerobics.
He goes to the health club.
He plays tennis.
He plays team sports.

B Books open. Tell students, "Now, watch and listen again. This time, circle the things you think Mark *really* does."

■ Play the sequence. Have students complete the task alone and then compare answers with a partner.

■ Ask if anyone needs to see the sequence again. Replay as needed, and then check answers around the class.

Answers
Mark *really* does the following things:
He gets up early.
He goes to the health club.
He plays tennis.

6 *WHAT'S YOUR OPINION?*

In this activity, students use adjectives in giving opinions about Anne and Mark.

■ Books open. Explain the task, and lead students through the four illustrations, explaining the meanings of the adjectives as needed.

■ *Pair work* Have students, working in pairs, complete the chart by choosing a word or words to describe Anne and a word or words to describe Mark.

■ Go over answers with the class, and encourage students to give reasons for their choices.

Possible answers
In general, Anne is friendly and polite, and Mark is friendly and pushy.

Follow-up

7 *INTERVIEW*

Through these communicative activities, students deepen their understanding of the topic by first writing questions about sports and exercise and then using these questions to conduct an interview with Mark or Anne.

A Books open. Explain the task, and read the questions given with students.

■ *Pair work* Have students work in pairs to write three additional questions about sports and exercise (e.g., "Do you go to a health club?" "Do you like aerobics?"). Circulate to check for accuracy.

B Books open. Explain the task, and have students change partners to conduct their interviews. Make sure students understand that they are to answer with information that is true for Mark or for Anne.

(procedure continues on next page)

■ Ask a few pairs to perform their interviews for the class.

Possible conversations

Interviewer: What kind of sports do you play?
Mark:　　　Well, I play most sports.
Interviewer: What's your favorite sport?
Mark:　　　Tennis. I'm a great tennis player . . .

Interviewer: Are you in good shape?
Anne:　　　Well, yes. I jog every morning.
Interviewer: Oh, how many miles do you jog?
Anne:　　　I usually jog about four or
　　　　　　five miles . . .

Optional activity

■ *Pair work* Books open or closed. Have students work in pairs to write five questions to ask either Anne or Mark about her or his morning in the park (e.g., "What time did you come here?" "Do you exercise every day?").

■ Have students form new pairs and ask and answer each other's questions with information that is true for Mark or for Anne. (10 minutes)

8 HOW ABOUT YOU?

These activities further develop students' understanding as they relate personal habits to what they have learned in the sequence.

A Books open. Explain the task, and then have each student complete the chart with information that is true for herself or himself (e.g., "I sometimes play volleyball after school." "I never go jogging in the morning." "I don't usually walk to work on the weekend.").

■ Circulate to help and check for accuracy, and then have students compare their answers with a partner.

B *Class activity* Books open. Explain the task, and tell students to ask classmates questions from Activity 1 of Exercise 7 to find out who likes to exercise and who doesn't. Encourage students to talk to as many classmates as possible.

■ Have students report back to the class. Record the information in a class chart on the board.

Language close-up

9 WHAT DID THEY SAY?

This cloze activity has students complete the first part of the conversation between Mark and Anne.

■ Books open. Have students, working individually or in pairs, fill in any blanks they can before watching the sequence.

■ Play this segment of the sequence through once. Have students work alone to check their predictions and fill in the blanks as they watch.

■ Have students compare answers with a partner and then watch again to check their answers.

■ Go over answers with the class, and replay this section as needed.

■ Model the conversation or, if you wish, do choral or individual repetition to prepare for pair work. Then have students practice the conversation in pairs.

Answers

Mark: Hi there. Nice **day**, isn't it?
Anne: Oh, yes, very **nice**.
Mark: Do you **often** come out here this **early**?
Anne: Usually. I like to stay in **shape**.
Mark: I do, too. I **usually** get up around
　　　five o'clock.
Anne: Oh, **really**?
Mark: Yeah. I **usually** start with some
　　　stretches. There's a **great** aerobics
　　　program on TV at **six**.
Anne: No **kidding**! I guess you really do **like** to
　　　stay in shape.
Mark: Hey, **three** days a **week** I go straight to
　　　my health club after **work**.

Optional activity

■ *Pair work* Books open. Have students work in pairs to write a possible conversation between Mark and the next person he approaches.

■ Have pairs read or act out their new conversations for the class. (10–15 minutes)

10 ADVERBS OF FREQUENCY

In these activities, students practice with adverbs of frequency, the grammatical focus of this sequence.

A Books open. Explain the task, and go over the example.

■ Have students complete the task and then compare answers with a partner.

■ Check answers around the class, and review as necessary.

Answers
1) I never get up before 5 A.M.
2) I usually don't have a big breakfast.
3) I sometimes play tennis after work.
4) I often take a long walk on the weekend.
5) I never watch TV.
6) I always jog in the morning.

B Books open. Explain the task. Have students work individually to complete the activity and then compare answers with a partner.

■ Check answers around the class, and accept all sentences that make sense.

Possible answers
1) I never get up before 5 A.M.
2) I always have a big breakfast.
3) I sometimes play tennis after work.
4) I never take a long walk on the weekend.
5) I often watch TV.
6) I never jog in the morning.

C Books open. Explain the task, and go over the adverbs of frequency listed, using them in example sentences as necessary.

■ Have students complete the sentences and then share them with a partner.

■ Check sentences around the class, and then ask several volunteers to share sentences with their classmates.

■ Make corrections, and review the adverbs of frequency as needed.

Optional activity

Pair work Books open. Have partners write five statements, using adverbs of frequency, that they think are true for Anne. (5 minutes)

Possible answers
I usually get up at 6 A.M.
I often jog with my friends.
I sometimes ride my bicycle to work.
I often do aerobics.
I exercise three times a week.

7 How was your trip to San Francisco?

Topics/functions: Describing past events; expressing opinions

Structures: Past tense

Summary

The sequence opens with Phyllis waiting for her friend Yoko, who is giving her a ride to work. When Yoko's car pulls up, Phyllis gets in, and Yoko asks about her trip to San Francisco. As Yoko continues to ask questions and Phyllis describes what she and her husband Bill did in San Francisco, the video sequence scene shows Phyllis and Bill there – riding a cable car, shopping at Ghirardelli Square, eating lunch at Fisherman's Wharf, walking in the Japanese Tea Garden in Golden Gate Park, and exploring Chinatown. The scene ends with the two women arriving at the office building where they work.

 Preview

1 CULTURE

In this sequence, Phyllis and Yoko ride to work together. They probably "carpool" every day, an arrangement in which they take turns driving each other to work. While the topic of car pools is not a focus of this unit, students may be interested in knowing that car pools are quite common in the United States and Canada as people try to save gas and other expenses and reduce traffic on busy city streets. In fact, many companies strongly encourage their employees to carpool, especially if parking spaces around their buildings are limited.

The culture preview in the Video Activity Book presents some interesting background information about San Francisco, the city described and depicted in this sequence.

■Books closed. Tell students that in this unit they will learn more about San Francisco, a famous city in California. Ask, "Do you know anything about San Francisco?" Have students share what they know before you go to the next step. If students are not familiar with San Francisco, prepare students to read the culture preview in the text by saying, "Well, let's learn about San Francisco."

■Books open. Have students read through the culture information silently and underline one new thing they learn about San Francisco. When they finish, ask, "What did you learn?" and have a few volunteers answer.

■Answer any content or vocabulary questions. Then have students work in pairs or small groups to answer the questions as you circulate around the class.

2 VOCABULARY Places in San Francisco

This activity introduces the names of famous places and attractions in San Francisco that students will see and hear described in the video.

■Books open. For each photo, ask students, "What do you see in this picture?" Do not have students name the scene but rather describe it, with sentences such as, "I see a bridge."

■*Pair work* Explain the task, and have students match the captions to the photos.

■Go over the answers with the class by holding up your book and asking, as you point to a photo, "What's this?" or "Where's this?" Have students call out answers.

Answers
1) A cable car
2) Fisherman's Wharf
3) Chinatown
4) Ghirardelli Square
5) The Japanese Tea Garden
6) The Golden Gate Bridge

3 GUESS THE STORY

In this activity, students prepare to watch the sequence by making predictions, based on visual information, about the things Phyllis and her husband see.

■ Books open. Have students work individually or in pairs to look at the photos in Exercise 2 on page 30 again, and mark an ✗ next to each thing they would like to see. Ask a few students to share opinions with the class.

■ Ask students to look at the photo, and explain that the sequence is about a professional woman in her mid-thirties who visits San Francisco with her husband. Then have students return to the photos in Exercise 2 and this time write a check (✓) next to the things they think the couple sees. Have students work alone to make predictions and then compare them with a partner.

■ Play the entire sequence without sound, as students watch and check their predictions.

■ Tell students that they will find out if their predictions are correct in the next activity.

Optional activity

Books closed. Play the sequence without the sound, stopping the video after each section that shows a place where Phyllis and her husband visit (Ghirardelli Square, Fisherman's Wharf, the Japanese Tea Garden, Chinatown). Have students list all the things they see in each place. (10 minutes)

Possible answers

Ghirardelli Square: stores, a fountain, chocolate, postcards, people, flowers

Fisherman's Wharf: food stands, a crab stand, people

Golden Gate Park: The Japanese Tea Garden, trees, plants, a footbridge

Chinatown: statues, people, shops, fruit, signs, restaurants, buildings

 Watch the video

4 GET THE PICTURE

In the first activity, students watch and listen to check the predictions they made in the preceding exercise. In the second activity, they watch and listen for the information needed to correct errors in Phyllis's travel diary.

A Books open. Explain the task, and make sure that students turn to Exercise 2 on page 30 to check their predictions as they watch the sequence.

■ Play the entire sequence with the sound on, as students complete the task. Then have selected students provide the answers, and replay the sequence as necessary.

Answers

The couple sees all the things pictured in Exercise 2 *except* the Golden Gate Bridge.

B Books open. Explain the task, and review the information in the travel diary, making sure students understand the sample correction under "Friday."

■ Books closed. Play the entire sequence with the sound on. Tell students to watch and listen for the things Phyllis and her husband did on Friday, on Saturday, and on Sunday.

■ Books open. Have students work alone to correct the errors in the travel diary, and then have students compare answers in pairs or small groups.

■ Ask if anyone needs to watch the sequence again, and replay if necessary before going over the answers with the class.

Answers

Friday: *sight-seeing* should be *work*
Saturday: *work* should be *sight-seeing*
Notes: *Fisherman's Wharf* should be *Chinatown*

5 WATCH FOR DETAILS

In this activity, students watch and listen for specific information about what Phyllis and her husband bought or did at the places they visited.

■ Books open. Explain the task, and lead students through the information in the chart. Have students, working individually or in pairs, predict the answers before watching.

■ Play the entire sequence with the sound on. Have students complete the task as they watch and then compare answers with a partner or around the class.

■ Check if anyone needs to watch the sequence again, and replay as needed.

Answers
1) They bought some postcards.
2) They had lunch.
3) They visited a tea garden.
4) They walked for hours.

Follow-up

6 A DAY IN SAN FRANCISCO

In this exercise, students first express their opinions and discuss the things in San Francisco they think are most interesting. Then they use the information they have learned about the city to plan an afternoon there. Since students will be working in small groups, they may need to negotiate and compromise as they make their plans.

A Books open. Lead students through the photos and have them read each caption.

■ *Group work* Explain the task, and then put students into groups of three or four. Before they begin, remind students that they must number the photos in order of interest as a group.

■ Ask students from various groups to say which of the places their groups think are most and least interesting – and why.

B Books open. Explain the task. Tell students that their group must decide where to visit or what to do.

■ Give the groups approximately 5 minutes to complete the task, and then ask each group to share their plans with the class.

Optional activities

A *Group work* Books open. Tell students, "I'm sorry, but you only have time to do two things in San Francisco. With your group, decide which two of the three activities you really want to do. You have three minutes."

■ Have groups share their plans with each other, and then say, "I'm sorry, but you'll only have enough time in San Francisco to do one thing. You have two minutes to decide. Go!"

■ When time is up, ask each group to share their final decision with the class. (10 minutes)

B *Group work* Books open. Have students plan a day trip for Phyllis and her husband to the city where your school is located. Follow the same procedure described in the preceding activity. (10 minutes)

7 WHAT'S YOUR OPINION?

In these activities, students relate their real-world knowledge and experience to what they have learned in this unit by talking about the things they like to do when visiting a new city.

A Books open. Explain the task, and lead students through the five items on the list.

■ *Pair work* Have students, working in pairs, number the five items in order of preference and then add three more items to the list (e.g., walk around, go to museums, go to a park).

■ Ask one student from each pair to say what they like to do most when visiting a new city, and ask other students to share what additional activities they listed.

■ Alternatively, have students work alone to rank the items, and then put students in groups and say, "This is a group trip. You all must agree on what you like to do. Work together until you all have the same order. Then add three more activities you all agree on."

B Books open. Explain the task, and model the sample conversation.

■ Have pairs of students work together, asking and answering questions similar to the example.

Language close-up

8 *WHAT DID THEY SAY?*

This cloze activity has students focus on specific language in the first part of the conversation between Yoko and Phyllis.

■ Books open. Have students, working individually or in pairs, read the conversation and fill in any blanks they can before watching the sequence. Then have pairs compare predictions around the class.

■ Play this segment of the video through once. Have students check their predictions and fill in the blanks as they watch.

■ Ask students to compare answers with a partner, and then have them watch the segment again to check their answers.

■ Check answers by having selected students read aloud one line of the dialogue at a time.

■ Model the dialogue or, if you wish, lead a choral or individual repetition of it before putting students into pairs to practice.

Answers
Yoko: Hi, Phyllis.
Phyllis: Hi, Yoko. **How** have you been?
Yoko: Oh, **fine**. How **about** you?
Phyllis: Great! Just **great**!
Yoko: So, **how** was your **trip** to San Francisco?
Phyllis: Fantastic! We really **enjoyed** it.
Yoko: Well, that **doesn't** surprise me. I love to **visit** San Francisco. Uh, so, your **husband** went with you?
Phyllis: Yes. I **worked** on Friday, and Bill had business to do in the **city**, too.
Yoko: Oh, that's **nice**. So, what did you do over the **weekend**?
Phyllis: We went **sight-seeing** together all day Saturday and Sunday **morning**.
Yoko: Oh, really? **Tell** me about it.

Optional activities

A *Pair work* Books open. Have students continue the conversation by taking turns playing the role of Phyllis and telling what she and her husband did in San Francisco. (5 minutes)

B *Pair work* Books closed. Have students talk about their own weekends. (5 minutes)

9 *PAST TENSE* Describing a trip

In these activities, students practice the simple past tense by filling in the correct verb forms in conversations from the sequence and by having similar conversations of their own.

A Books open. Explain the task, and have students work alone to silently read through each conversation and fill in the correct verb forms.

■ Then have students compare answers with a partner or around the class.

■ Check answers around the class, and review the past tense as necessary.

■ Have students work in pairs to practice the conversations.

Answers
1) Yoko: Tell me about your trip to San Francisco.
   Phyllis: Well, we did a lot of interesting things. Naturally, we started Saturday morning with a ride on a cable car.
   Yoko: Naturally! And then?
   Phyllis: Then we went straight to Ghirardelli Square to do some shopping.
   Yoko: Isn't it wonderful? I went there the last time I was in San Francisco.
2) Yoko: Did you visit Alcatraz Island?
   Phyllis: No, we didn't have time.
   Yoko: Oh, what did you do then?
   Phyllis: We took a cab to Golden Gate Park.
   Yoko: Great! Did you see the Japanese Tea Garden?
   Phyllis: Oh, yes, it was really beautiful. But, to tell the truth, the thing we liked best was Chinatown.

(procedure continues on next page)

B *Pair work* Books open. Explain the task, and read through the model conversation with students. Then have students form pairs and have similar conversations.

■ Circulate to help, and when students seem satisfied, either have them change partners to have another conversation or have several pairs perform their conversations for the class.

Optional activity

■ *Group work* Books closed. Have students form groups of five or six. Then say, "You are going to tell the story of a trip to San Francisco. Each of you must repeat what the students in front of you said and then add a sentence of your own."

■ Demonstrate with the class:
A: We went to San Francisco and we saw the Japanese Tea Garden.
B: We went to San Francisco and we saw the Japanese Tea Garden and bought some postcards . . .

■ Ask a few students to provide example sentences, and then have the groups continue on their own.

■ Have groups continue until each group member has a turn. (10 minutes)

8 Are you sure it's all right?

Topics/functions: Describing locations; inviting

Structures: Prepositions of location; Wh-questions

Summary

The sequence opens with Sandy, Bill, and Pat in a car on their way to a party at Katy's house. Sandy is worried because Katy didn't actually invite her or Pat to the party, but Bill tells her that it's OK since it's an informal party. Bill doesn't know Katy's address, but he remembers some of the stores and other buildings in her neighborhood and uses their locations to give Pat, who is driving, directions. When they finally get to Katy's apartment building, Sandy is worried that they have arrived too late. Bill knocks on the door, and as they wait for Katy to open her door, Sandy says she is surprised they don't hear any music. Just then Katy opens the door and greets them, but she seems surprised. Bill asks if they are too late for the party, and Katy replies, "Oh, no. Actually you're a little early. The party is next Friday." Katy invites the three unexpected guests in anyway.

Preview

1 CULTURE

In the video, Sandy is worried about whether it is really all right for her and Pat to go to Katy's party since they were not specifically invited. Bill assures her that it is OK since the party is informal. If Katy's party were a formal one, however, it would not be proper for Bill to bring uninvited guests along with him.

Rules and customs regarding invitations vary widely from culture to culture. The culture preview in the Video Activity Book presents students with some simple rules for attending a dinner or party at someone's home in the United States and Canada.

■ Books closed. Ask students, "In your culture, if someone invites you to dinner, is it OK to bring another person with you?" Have students indicate yes or no by raising their hands. Then ask, "Is it OK to bring someone with you to an informal party?" If necessary, explain the term *informal*, and again have students respond by raising their hands.

■ Books open. Ask students to silently read the culture information to see whether the rules for invitations in the United States and Canada are similar to the rules in their culture.

■ Have students talk about the questions in pairs, and then have selected pairs share their answers with the class.

Optional activity

■ *Group work* Books open or closed. Have students from the same culture form small groups and then list rules – in their culture – for being invited to someone's home. Help students get started by giving additional examples of rules in the United States and Canada (e.g., "You shouldn't be late for dinner." "You don't have to bring a gift, but it's always a nice thing to do.").

■ Have groups compare rules around the class. (5 minutes)

2 *VOCABULARY* Places

In this activity, students practice working with place names and location terms presented in the sequence.

■ Books open. Explain the task, and review the example. Lead students through the rest of the sentences, and give additional examples if necessary.

■ *Pair work* Have students, working in pairs, complete the task and then compare their answers with another pair.

■ Check answers around the class, and review the location terms as necessary.

Answers

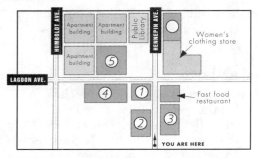

Optional activity

■ Books closed. Prepare a simple map of the area around your school or classroom on the board, and label several buildings. Write a model question-answer exchange on the board, such as the following:
A: What's across the street from the school?
B: A drugstore.

■ *Pair work* Have students work in pairs to ask and answer questions about the map following the model provided. (5 minutes)

3 *GUESS THE STORY*

In this activity, students watch the beginning of the sequence in order to predict what happens as the story progresses.

■ Books open. Ask students to look at the photo of Bill, Pat, and Sandy, and explain that these three friends are on their way to a party.

■ Ask students, "What do you think happens in the story?" and read through the three possibilities with them. (Note: You may want students to make a guess at this point based on the information in the culture box and the focus of the vocabulary exercise.)

■ Books closed. Play the first minute of the sequence with the sound off (stop the sequence while Pat, Sandy, and Bill are still shown driving in the car).

■ Books open. Have students work alone to make their predictions.

■ Check answers around the class, and replay this segment of the video if needed.

■ At this point, do not tell students which answer is correct (They go on the wrong day.), but explain that the answer will become clear as they continue to work with the sequence.

Optional activities

A Books closed. Have students watch the beginning of the sequence with the sound off again and list the things they can see in Katy's neighborhood (e.g., stores, street signs, traffic lights, people). (5 minutes)

B *Pair work* Books closed. Play the sequence from the point where Katy answers the door to the end with the sound off, and have pairs of students write what they think Bill and Katy say to each other. (10 minutes)

Watch the video

4 GET THE PICTURE

In the first activity, students watch and listen for the information needed to answer four general questions about the story. In the second activity, students check the predictions they made in Exercise 3 by watching the entire sequence with the sound on.

A Books open. Ask students to look at the photos of the four characters, and lead them through the four questions.

■ Have students try to answer any questions they can before viewing and then compare predictions with a partner.

■ Tell students, "We are going to watch the video with the sound on. Watch and listen for the answers to the questions."

■ Play the entire sequence with the sound on, with students checking their predictions and marking the correct answers as they watch.

■ Have students compare answers with a partner. Then check answers around the class, and replay the sequence if necessary.

Answers
1) Katy
2) Bill
3) Pat, Sandy
4) Bill

B Books open. Read the two questions with students, and then have them form pairs or small groups to check their predictions from Exercise 3. If necessary, replay the sequence with the sound on.

■ Have the pairs or small groups share their answers with the class.

5 WATCH FOR DETAILS

In this activity, students focus more closely on details in the sequence in order to correct mistakes in a summary of the story.

■ Books open. Explain the task, and read through the summary with students. Review the sample correction, and make sure they understand that the summary contains other mistakes that they need to correct.

■ Have students work alone to correct any errors they can before watching the sequence and then compare their predictions with a partner.

■ Books closed. Play the entire sequence with the sound on.

■ Books open. Have students work alone to check their predictions and to correct other mistakes in the summary.

■ Ask students to compare answers around the class. Circulate and check for accuracy. Replay the sequence if necessary before giving the corrected version of the summary.

Answers
Pat, Bill, and **Sandy** are going to a party at **Katy's** apartment. The party is very **informal**. **Bill** doesn't remember the exact address, but he remembers there's a **movie theater** just before you turn. When they arrive, they don't hear any music. It's a little **early**. The party **is next** week.

6 *WHAT'S YOUR OPINION?*

In this activity, students give their opinions about the situation and the characters' feelings.

■ Books open. Explain the task, and lead students through the three questions and the possible answers. Discuss any vocabulary or content questions.

■ *Pair work* Have students work in pairs to answer the questions, and then have the pairs form small groups to compare and discuss answers.

■ Ask several students to share their answers and ideas with the class.

Answers

Accept all answers if students can support them with details from the video. In general, the following answers are the most accurate.
1) Yes, it's fine.
2) surprised
3) embarrassed

Optional activity

Group work Books open or closed. Have groups list adjectives to describe how Bill feels when he realizes his mistake (e.g., silly, embarrassed) and how he feels when Katy invites them in (e.g., relieved, happy, still embarrassed). (5 minutes)

Follow-up

7 *INVITING*

In this activity, students practice inviting, a functional focus of the sequence.

■ Books open. Read through the instructions with the class, and go over the four illustrations and the accompanying captions.

■ Model the conversation, and/or select two students to model it with you.

■ *Group work* Have students form small groups to practice the conversation. Alternatively, you might wish to have all the students walk around, with each student practicing the conversation several times – each time with a different classmate.

■ Bring the class back together after about 5 minutes, and have selected groups of three perform the conversation for the class.

8 *ROLE PLAY* A surprise guest

These activities give students the chance to demonstrate and strengthen comprehension and be creative by acting out a scene from the video and developing two alternate endings.

A Books open. Lead students through the directions, and make sure they understand that their task is to act out the situation three times.

■ Put students into groups of four. Then, for each group, assign each member the role of one of the four characters.

■ *Group work* Play the sequence from the scene where Bill knocks on Katy's door until the end, and then have groups stand and act out the conversation, staying as close to the action and dialogue in the video as possible.

■ When all the groups are finished, clap your hands and say, "Now, act it out again. This time, Katy is busy and doesn't want company." Give students 3–5 minutes to act out this situation.

Responses Katy might give

I'm sorry. I'm busy right now . . .
I'm studying for a big test I have to take tomorrow.
I'm cleaning my apartment.

■ Now, ask the groups to sit down and, in 5–10 minutes, develop and act out a new ending for the story.

B Books closed. When time is up, have each group perform for the class. After the performances, have the class vote on the "best" new ending. Encourage students to give reasons for choosing particular endings.

Language close-up

9 WHAT DID THEY SAY?

This cloze activity has students complete part of the conversation among Pat, Bill, and Sandy.

- Books open. Have students, working individually or in pairs, fill in any blanks they can before watching the sequence.

- Play this segment of the sequence. Have students work alone to check predictions and fill in the blanks as they watch.

- Have students compare answers with a partner and then watch the segment again to check their answers.

- Check answers with the class, and then replay the sequence so that students can hear the answers in context.

- Model the conversation or lead a choral or individual repetition before putting students into groups of three to practice it.

Answers
Pat: OK. Well, we're at the **corner** of 31st Street. **Now** what?

Bill: Well, I don't remember her **address**, but I know she lives **near** here.

Pat: Fine. But do I go **left**, right, or straight **ahead**?

Bill: **Straight** ahead. . . . I remember there's a **movie** theater just before you **turn**.

Pat: Hey, is **that** it?

Bill: No, I **don't** think so. . . . There was a coffee shop **next** door and a drugstore **across** the street.

Sandy: Oh, I don't see a **drugstore**. Well, there's a Vietnamese **restaurant** . . . with a bookstore **next** to it.

Pat: Yeah, and no **coffee** shop either. Hey, look! There's another movie theater up ahead on the **left**.

Bill: Great! **There's** a drugstore.

Optional activity

Group work Books open. Have students practice the conversation again in groups of three. Tell them that Pat and Sandy are angry at Bill because they think he doesn't really know where Katy lives. (5 minutes)

10 LOCATIONS

In these activities, students ask Wh-questions and practice with prepositions of location, the grammatical focus of the unit.

A Books open. Have students look at the map of Katy's neighborhood. Then review the sample question and answer, and read the rest of the questions with them.

- Have students work alone to complete the task, and then put students in pairs to take turns asking and answering the questions.

Possible answers
1) It's across from the Vietnamese restaurant.
2) It's next to the Vietnamese restaurant.
3) It's near Border's Book Shop.
4) It's on the corner of Lake Street and Hennepin Avenue.
5) It's on Hennepin Avenue.

B *Pair work* Books open. Have each pair write five questions about places near their school, following the models provided in the preceding activity.

- Have students form new pairs and then take turns asking and answering each other's questions.

Optional activity

- *Pair work* Books open or closed. Have students work in pairs to draw a map of the neighborhood around the school – but with three buildings in the wrong places. Then have each pair write three false statements about the places on the map.

- Have pairs exchange maps and statements, and correct each other's work. (10 minutes)

In a suburban home

Preview

1 VOCABULARY Guess the rooms of a house

This activity prepares students for working with the language presented in the documentary by introducing the vocabulary for rooms of a house.

- Books open. Explain the task, and model the names of the rooms.
- **Pair work** Ask students to look at the photos, and then have them work in pairs to match the words and the photos.
- Have students compare answers in small groups, and then explain to students that they will have a chance to check their answers when they watch the documentary.

Answers
1) kitchen
2) dining room
3) living room
4) family room
5) guest room
6) child's bedroom

Optional activity

- Books closed. Have students watch the documentary without the sound and then make predictions about what each of the rooms shown is used for and who in the family uses that room the most.
- Check predictions around the class, but be careful not to give away the answers at this point. (5 minutes)

Watch the video

2 GET THE PICTURE

In the first activity, students watch and listen to check the predictions they made in Exercise 1. In the second activity, they watch and listen to find out what the Bartletts do in the kitchen, in the dining room, and in the family room.

A Books open. Tell students that they will watch the documentary to check their answers in Exercise 1.

- Play the entire sequence, while students check and correct their answers as they watch.
- Have students compare answers with a partner and then check answers as a class.

B Books open. Explain the task, and read through the sentence stems with the class.

- If you wish, have students work in pairs to predict the answers before viewing.
- Play the documentary, and have students work alone to complete the sentences.
- Ask students to compare answers with a partner. Replay the video if necessary for clarification.
- Go over the answers with the class.

Possible answers
1) In the kitchen, they eat family meals.
2) In the dining room, they entertain guests and have special family meals.
3) In the family room, they watch TV and play games.

3 WATCH FOR DETAILS

In this activity, students focus more closely on details in the documentary in order to list the things they see in each room of the house.

- Books open. Explain to students that they are going to watch the documentary again and that this time they should list the things they see in each of the eight rooms of the Bartlett house.
- Play the entire sequence with the sound on or off. As they watch, have students work alone to list the items they see in each room.
- Put students into groups of five or six to compare answers.

■Have students check their answers by playing the documentary again and freezing the picture as each room is shown. Point out objects in the frame and ask, "What's this? Did you list it?" Continue in this manner until you have gone through all the rooms.

Possible answers

1) the kitchen: sink, stove, refrigerator, cabinets, table, chairs, coffee machine, telephone
2) the dining room: table, chairs, mirror, light, plant
3) the living room: coffee table, chairs, couch, fireplace, pictures
4) Matthew's room: bed, desk, chair, pillows, stuffed animals, posters
5) the guest room: bed, dresser, pictures, TV
6) Daniel's room: bed, desk, TV, clock, books, posters, trophies, bookshelves
7) the large bedroom: bed, dresser, lamp, clock, pictures, pillows, TV
8) the family room: couch, chair, fireplace, TV, game

4 WHAT'S YOUR OPINION?

In this activity, students give their opinions about what they like or dislike about the Bartlett home and talk about how this home differs from typical homes in their countries.

■Books open. Explain the task, and read through the discussion questions before having students form pairs.

■ *Pair work* Give pairs about 5 minutes to discuss the questions, and then bring students back together to share answers as a class.

Optional activity

Group work Books open. Have students work in groups of three or four – for about 5 minutes – to make a list of adjectives to describe the Bartlett home. When time is up, bring the class together, and compile a master list of adjectives on the board. (10 minutes)

Possible answers
lovely, new, modern, nice, big, beautiful, clean, neat, bright, colorful, comfortable, warm

 *Follow-up*

5 YOUR HOME

In this activity, students extend and personalize the information by interviewing classmates about their homes or apartments.

■Books open. Explain the task, and read through the list of questions with the class.

■Have students work in pairs to add to the list two or three questions that they would like to ask, while you circulate and check for accuracy.

■ *Group work* Divide the class into groups of five or six, and have students take turns asking other groups members about their homes.

■Bring the class back together, and ask each group to share with the class the most interesting thing they learned about a group member's home.

Optional activity

■ *Pair work* Have students work in pairs to draw and label layouts of each other's homes: Students sit back to back and take turns asking questions about each other's home. They do their drawings based on the answers.

■When both students have finished their drawings, have them exchange the drawings to check for accuracy. (10–15 minutes)

9 Help is coming.

| **Topics/functions:** Describing physical appearance; describing what people are doing |
| **Structures:** Present continuous |

Summary

The sequence opens at dusk in a suburban neighborhood. Dave and Sarah Johnson are sitting in their living room reading. Over Dave's shoulder we see the newspaper headline: "Two men escape from prison in gray van." Dave mentions the escape to Sarah, who gets up and looks out the window. She notices that a minivan with two men in it is parked in front of the house. She tells Dave and he asks questions about the van and the men. Worried that these are the men who escaped from prison, Dave decides to call the police when the men start to approach the house. When he returns to tell Sarah that help is coming, Sarah suddenly realizes that one of the men is Dave's cousin George. Sarah invites him in and George tells them that he and his son Don, who Dave and Sarah have not seen since he was a baby, are traveling through town and decided to say hello. The sequence ends with Dave feeling silly as he realizes it is too late to stop the police from coming – police sirens can be heard approaching.

Preview

1 CULTURE

The culture preview in the Video Activity Book presents information about how people in the United States and Canada protect their homes against crime and prepares students to work with the story by building up a sense of anticipation.

■ Books closed. Tell students, "We are going to look at a list of ways that people can protect their homes against crime. What do you think will be on the list?" Give an example, and ask students to

suggest a few other possibilities. Write the suggestions on the board. (Note: You may want to limit the discussion at this point, since students will have a chance for further discussion when they work with the questions in the culture preview.)

■ Books open. Have students read the culture preview silently to see if any of the suggestions they made are included in it.

■ Ask selected students to name ways people in the United States and Canada protect their homes that are described in the culture information and have not been mentioned yet.

■ Put students into pairs or small groups to answer the questions.

■ Ask groups to share their responses with the class.

2 VOCABULARY Physical appearance

These activities introduce and practice vocabulary that can be used to describe people's physical appearances, a functional focus of the sequence.

A *Pair work* Books open. Explain the task, and present the new vocabulary. Then have pairs put the words in the appropriate columns in the chart and add two more words or phrases.

■ Ask pairs to compare their new words and phrases around the class. Then have students call out new words, and list them on the board.

Answers

Age	Height	Hair
early forties	short	short
late forties	tall	long
elderly		curly
		blond
		bald

Additional words

Age	Height	Hair
twenties	medium	straight
thirties		wavy

B *Pair work* Books open. Ask students to look at the photo of the man, Dave, and the woman, Sarah. Then explain the task, and have pairs list two ways to describe each of them. Encourage students to use words and phrases from the preceding activity.

■ Have students compare answers around the class.

Possible answers

The man	*The woman*
late forties	early forties
bald	curly blonde hair

Optional activity

Books open or closed. Fast forward to the segment of the video in which the two men, George and Don, enter the house. Show this scene with the sound off, and if possible freeze the frame. Ask students to list two words or phrases to describe each of these men. (5 minutes)

Possible answers

George	*Don*
short	tall
brown hair	blond hair
late forties	early twenties

3 GUESS THE STORY

In this activity, students prepare to watch the sequence by using visual information to predict what happens in the story.

■ Books open. Explain the task. Play the first minute of the video with the sound off (until just after Sarah looks out the window – and the minivan is shown for the first time), as students watch and write down their predictions.

■ Ask a few students to share their predictions with the class, and accept all answers at this point. Explain that they will find out more in the next activity.

Optional activity

Books closed. Play the entire sequence with the sound off (in slow motion if possible) and have students, working individually or in pairs, list the things they see Dave and Sarah doing and then compare answers with other students. (10 minutes)

Possible answers

Dave: Dave's reading the paper. He's talking to Sarah. He's getting up from the couch. He's opening the door. He's talking to the men. He's making a telephone call.

Sarah: Sarah's reading a book. She's picking up her coffee cup. She's talking to Dave. She's walking to the window. She's looking out the window. She's waving to the men to come into the house. She's talking to the men.

 Watch the video

4 GET THE PICTURE

In this activity, students watch and listen to check the predictions they made in Exercise 3 and to determine what really happens in the sequence.

■ Books open. Explain the task, and lead students through the possible choices.

■ Books closed. Play the entire sequence with the sound on.

■ Books open. Have students choose their answers and then compare with neighboring students.

■ Circulate to check answers, and replay the sequence if necessary before giving the answer (Dave's cousin comes to visit.).

5 *WATCH FOR DETAILS*

In this activity, students focus more closely on details in the sequence by watching and listening to put events in the correct order.

■ Books open. Explain the task, and then have students, working individually or in pairs, predict the correct order of the pictures before watching the sequence. (Note: Students should not read the accompanying sentences at this point.) Have students compare their predictions with each other.

■ Play the entire sequence with the sound on. As they watch, have students check and correct their predictions.

■ In pairs, have students compare answers and then work together to match the sentences and the pictures.

■ Check answers around the class.

Answers (from left to right)

6 The men are introducing themselves to Sarah and Dave.
4 The men are standing in the driveway.
5 Dave is calling the police.
1 Sarah and Dave are reading.
3 The men are getting out of the minivan.
2 Sarah is looking at the minivan.

Optional activity

■ *Class activity* Books closed. Fast forward the sequence from the beginning. From the moment you start fast forwarding, have students count down from three (3, 2, 1). When they reach number one, stop the video and freeze the frame. Then point to a student and ask, "What's happening here?" Have the student describe what is happening using the present continuous.

■ Repeat the process until you reach the end of the sequence. As you proceed, you might want to have the student who just answered select the next student to answer. (10 minutes)

6 *DESCRIBING SOMEONE*

In these activities, students use information from the sequence to describe George and Don. The Video Activity Book presents useful words and phrases for giving physical descriptions of people.

A Books open. Have students look at the photos of George and Don, and ask a few students to call out adjectives to describe one or the other of the men.

■ Explain the task, and have students, working individually or in pairs, complete the chart.

■ After a minute or two, ask students if they would like to watch the segment again in order to refresh their memories. Replay the sequence from the point where the two men enter the house.

■ Have students compare answers with a partner, and then check answers around the class.

Answers

George	Don
1) forties	twenties
2) brown	blond
3) short	tall
4) short-sleeved	long-sleeved
5) no hat	baseball cap
glasses	no glasses

B Books open. Have students, working individually or in pairs, add some descriptive details about George and Don. If students seem unsure as to what they can add, replay the sequence from the point where the two men enter the house and tell them to watch and listen for the following: type of voice (deep, loud, soft), weight (heavy, thin, medium), length of hair (long, short, medium, bald), personality (shy, friendly).

■ Replay the sequence again as students work. Then have them compare answers with a partner.

Follow-up

7 THE RIGHT DECISION?

In this activity, students give opinions about the best thing to do in a situation similar to Sarah and Dave's.

■ Books open. Explain the task, and lead students through the choices listed. Make it clear to students that if they select "other," they should specify what it is they would do.

■ ***Pair work*** Put the students into pairs to decide, and then bring students together. Ask selected pairs to share their answers, and encourage them to give reasons for their choices.

Optional activity

■ Books open or closed. Tell the class to imagine that they are the police officers who have just arrived at Sarah and Dave's house. Ask students, "If you were the police officers, what would you do? Laugh? Be angry? Arrest George and Don?"

■ ***Pair work*** Put the students into pairs to decide, and then bring students together. Ask selected pairs to share their answers, and encourage them to give reasons for their choices. (10 minutes)

8 WHAT HAPPENS NEXT?

These extension activities encourage students to be creative in writing and acting out a conversation between Dave, Sarah, and the police officers.

A *Group work* Books open. Explain the task, and put students into groups of four to write a possible conversation among Dave, Sarah, and the police officers. (Note: You may want to set a time limit of 5–10 minutes for this.)

B *Class activity* Books closed. Have the groups practice and then act out their conversations for the class. If appropriate, have the class vote for the "best" performance.

Optional activity

Pair work Books open or closed. Put students into pairs to write a conversation that might take place between George and Don after they leave Dave and Sarah's house. Follow the procedure outlined in the preceding activity. (10 minutes)

Language close-up

9 WHAT DID THEY SAY?

In this cloze activity, students focus their attention on specific language used by Dave and Sarah in the opening scenes of the sequence.

■ Books open. Have students fill in any blanks they can before watching the video.

■ Play this segment of the video through once, while students work alone to fill in the missing words and check their predictions.

■ Ask if anyone needs to watch the video again, and replay as necessary.

■ Check answers around the class, and replay the segment again as needed.

■ Model the conversation or, if you wish, lead a choral or individual repetition of it. Then put students into pairs to practice the conversation.

Answers
Sarah: Would you **like** another cup of **coffee**?
Dave: **No**, thanks. I don't **think** so.
Sarah: Is there anything **interesting** in the **paper**?
Dave: Well, there's something about a **prison** escape.
Sarah: Oh, really?
Dave: Yeah. A couple of **guys** escaped from the state prison in a **gray** van.
Sarah: Hmm . . . **Do** we know **anyone** with a minivan?
Dave: A minivan? What **color** is it?
Sarah: I **don't** know. Light **blue**, maybe, or **gray**. I can't **see** very well.
Dave: Where is this **van**?
Sarah: It's parked right in **front** of the **house**. And there are **two** guys in it.

(see next page for an optional activity)

Optional activity

Pair work Books closed. Have students close their books and work in pairs to act out the conversation between Sarah and Dave. Tell students that they do not have to use their exact words, but should try to follow their actions as closely as possible. (5 minutes)

10 MODIFIERS WITH PARTICIPLES AND PREPOSITIONS

In the first activity, students use modifiers with participles and prepositions to identify Sarah, Dave, George, and Don through the clothes they are wearing. In the second activity, students have the chance to make sentences of their own about Sarah, Dave, George, and Don.

A Books open. Explain the task, and go over the example. Have students match the information in the three columns and check their answers with a partner. Replay segments of the sequence, if necessary.

■ Ask selected students to describe what is happening in the photos, and review the grammar as necessary.

Answers
Sarah is the blonde woman wearing a blue T-shirt.
Dave is the bald man wearing a green shirt.
George is the heavy one with glasses.
Don is the young one holding his hat.

B **Pair work** Books open. Have students look at the other photos on page 41, or play the scene towards the end of this sequence in which George and Don enter Sarah and Dave's house, and Sarah, Dave, George, and Don can all be seen. Then have students work in pairs to form additional sentences about the characters.

Possible answers
Dave is the one wearing white pants.
Don is the tall one wearing blue jeans.
Sarah is the woman with curly blonde hair.

Optional activity

Pair work Books closed. Put students in pairs, and play the entire sequence with the sound off (in slow motion if possible). Have students take turns describing to their partner what is happening. (5 minutes)

11 DESCRIBING SOMEONE

These extension activities conclude the unit by having students describe their classmates.

A **Pair work** Books open. Explain the task, and review the example. Then put students into pairs to ask and answer questions about classmates. Students should take turns describing a classmate while their partner guesses who is being described.

■ After each pair member has had a chance to describe at least one person, ask a few students to describe someone for the class.

B Books open. Have students work alone to write three true and two false sentences that describe classmates.

■ **Pair work** Have students take turns reading their sentences to a partner, who decides whether each sentence is true or false.

■ Ask several pairs to share their "best" sentences with the class.

Optional activity

■ Books open or closed. Have each student choose one of the four characters in the video and write five sentences to describe this person.

Possible answers

Dave: He's in his forties. He's almost bald. He's quite tall. He looks worried. He's wearing a green short-sleeved shirt and tan pants.

Sarah: She's in her early forties. She has curly blonde hair and brown eyes. She looks worried. She's wearing a blue short-sleeved shirt and tan pants.

George: He's in his late forties. He's short. He has brown hair, and he's wearing glasses. He's wearing a blue short-sleeved shirt. He's smiling, and he looks friendly.

Don: He's in his twenties. He's tall. He has blond hair, and he's wearing a baseball cap. He's wearing jeans and a blue long-sleeved shirt. He's smiling, and he looks friendly.

■ **Pair work** Have students, in pairs, take turns reading their sentences and guessing who is being described. (5 minutes)

10 Sorry I'm late.

Topic/functions: Telling a story

Structures: Present perfect; connecting words: *first*, *after that*, *next*, *then*, and *finally*

Summary

The sequence opens with Marie sitting alone in a restaurant. It is clear that she is waiting for someone who is late. When Tom finally arrives, he tells Marie what happened to him. As he describes the following events, the video shows what is happening. First, because he was late leaving his apartment, he was in a hurry. As he was about to drive away, he realized that he had left his wallet in the house. When he went to get his wallet, he locked his keys in the car and had to call a locksmith to come and open the car for him. When Marie asks Tom how much he had to pay the locksmith, he realizes that now he has left his wallet in the car. Marie tells Tom not to worry. She says, "You've had a hard day, and it's my turn to pay anyway."

 **Preview**

1 CULTURE

In the video sequence, Marie has to wait a long time before Tom finally arrives. In a recent survey, the majority of people from the United States and Canada questioned said they would wait no longer than 30 minutes for a friend who was late. The culture preview in the Video Activity Book introduces the topic of the sequence by presenting attitudes in the United States and Canada about being on time.

■ Books closed. Ask students, "Is it very important to be on time in your culture?" Have students respond by raising their hands to indicate "yes." Then ask, "What time should you arrive for a twelve o'clock class?" Solicit answers from several students, and then write the following situations on the board:
business appointment
meeting with a friend
dinner with someone
informal party

■ Say, "These events all start at six o'clock. What time should you arrive for each event?" In pairs, have students talk about and write down their answers.

■ Ask several students to share their answers with the class, and explain that ideas about being on time vary from culture to culture.

■ Books open. Have students read through the culture preview silently and compare their answers with the information presented.

■ Review the culture information with the class by asking selected students, "What time should you arrive for a business appointment in the United States and Canada? In your culture?" Follow the same procedure for the three other situations, and then put students into small groups to work with the questions.

■ Bring the class back together, and ask several students to share their answers.

Optional activity

■ Books open or closed. Ask students how many minutes they would wait for the following people if they were late: business associate, casual friend, close friend, teacher.

■ *Pair work* Put students into pairs to discuss these situations, and then have selected pairs share their answers with the class. (Though the times would vary, most people from the United States and Canada would commonly wait 15 minutes for a business associate or casual friend and 30 minutes for a close friend. In U.S. colleges, students would wait approximately 15 minutes for a professor.) (5 minutes)

2 VOCABULARY *Past tense of verbs*

In this activity, students practice and review
the past tense of various verbs presented in
the sequence.

■ *Pair work* Books open. Explain the task, and
review the example. Provide additional examples
if necessary. Have students work in pairs to
complete the chart and then compare answers
with a new partner or a neighboring student.

■ Check answers around the class, and review the
past tense of these verbs as needed. (Note: It
should not be necessary to expand further on the
past tense at this point.)

Answers

called	locked
did	opened
found	paid
got	remembered
went	sent
left	started

Optional activities

A *Pair work* Books open. Have each pair create
a story using eight to ten of the verbs in the past
tense from the chart. (10 minutes)

Possible story

Yesterday I **went** shopping. It was a nice day, so I
rode my bicycle. I **locked** my bike near the store
and **went** inside. When I **got** back to my bike, I
remembered that the key to the lock was on the
kitchen table at home! I **found** a phone booth
and **called** my house. Nobody was home. I
started walking home to get the key. Finally, I
arrived. But where was my house key? I **left** it on
the kitchen table, too! Luckily, just then my
brother came home and **opened** the door.

B Books open. Play the entire sequence with the
picture off, and have students check the past
tense of the verbs in the chart as they hear them.
(Note: Each of the verbs in the past tense is used
at least once in the sequence.) (5 minutes)

3 GUESS THE STORY

In this activity, students prepare to watch
the sequence by using visual information to
make predictions about what happens to Tom
and Marie.

■ Books open. Have students look at the photo.
Say, "This is Tom and this is Marie. What do you
think happened?" Lead students through the
four choices, and have them silently predict
the answers.

■ Tell students, "Now we are going to watch the
beginning of the video without sound. What
happens to Tom and Marie? Check your answers
as you watch."

■ Play the first minute of the sequence with the
sound off (until Tom is shown having locked his
keys in his car). Have students work alone to
check their predictions as they watch and then
compare them with a partner.

■ Check predictions around the class, and tell
students that they will find out the answers when
they watch the entire sequence (the man arrived
very late for dinner; the man didn't have his
wallet; the woman paid for dinner).

Optional activity

Pair work Play the sequence with the sound off
until the point where Tom is shown calling
someone on the telephone. Have students work in
pairs to write the first four lines of a possible
conversation between Tom and Marie after Tom
enters the restaurant. Circulate and check for
accuracy, and then have selected pairs read their
conversations to the class. (10 minutes)

Possible conversation

Tom: I'm sorry I'm late, Marie.
Marie: What happened?
Tom: I locked my keys in my car.
Marie: It's OK. Don't worry.

Watch the video

4 GET THE PICTURE

In this activity, students watch and listen to the entire sequence to answer questions about three main events in the story.

■ Books open. Explain the task by leading students through the three questions and then saying, "Now we will watch the sequence with the sound on to find the answer to each question."

■ Play the entire sequence with the sound on. Have students work alone to answer the questions while viewing and then compare answers with a partner.

■ Ask the class if they need to watch any part of the sequence again to answer the questions. Play the requested sections again before checking answers around the class.

Answers
1) He locked his keys in it.
2) He left it in the car.
3) Marie paid.

5 WATCH FOR DETAILS

In these activities, students focus more closely on details in the sequence by watching and listening in order to put events in the proper order and to describe two additional events in the story.

A Books open. Explain the task, and have students work alone to predict the proper order of the pictures before watching the sequence. (Note: Students should not read the accompanying statements at this point.)

■ Have students compare predictions with a partner. Then play the sequence through with the sound on so that students can check and correct their predictions.

■ Have students work alone to write the correct sentence under each picture. Ask students to compare answers with their neighbors, and then check answers around the class.

Answers (from left to right)
5 Tom called a lock service.
3 Tom saw his keys inside the car.
2 Tom remembered his wallet was in the house.
1 Tom left the house and started his car.
4 Tom tried to call Marie.
6 Tom remembered his wallet was in the car.

B *Pair work* Books open. Have students work in pairs to list two additional events that happened in the sequence. If necessary, replay the sequence again.

■ Check answers around the class, and ask several pairs to share one of the additional events they listed.

Possible answers
Tom looked in the phone book to find a lock service.
Tom paid the man from the lock service.

6 WHAT'S YOUR OPINION?

In this activity, students express opinions by choosing adjectives that they think describe Tom and Marie.

■ Books open. Explain the task, and review the meaning of each adjective in the chart.

■ *Pair work* Have pairs share their opinions and work together to complete the chart. Then have pairs compare their choices with another pair.

■ Have various students share answers with the class. As they do so, ask the other students to agree or disagree and to give reasons for their opinions when possible.

Possible answers
Tom: angry (at himself), upset, tired, embarrassed, worried
Marie: understanding, worried

Follow-up

7 QUESTION GAME

In these activities, students write, ask, and answer past-tense questions about the story to clarify their understanding of the events.

A Books open. Explain the task by first leading students through the two example questions and soliciting answers. Then have students work alone to write three additional questions. (Note: If you wish, replay the sequence as students work to refresh their memory.)

Answers
1) He remembered that he didn't have any money with him.
2) Tom locked his keys in his car when he went back to his apartment.

Additional possible questions and answers
Who did Tom try to call? (He tried to call Marie.)
How did Tom get his keys from the car? (He called a lock service. / A man from a lock service came and unlocked the car.)
Where did Tom leave his wallet the second time? (He left it in his car.)

B *Pair work* Books open. Circulate to check for accuracy, and then put students into pairs to ask and answer each other's questions.

8 TELL THE STORY

In this activity, students use connecting words to tell Tom and Marie's story in their own words.

■ Books open. Explain the task, and, if necessary, work with students to create some example sentences, using connecting words, about events in the story. If necessary, refer students back to the events listed in Exercise 5 on page 45.

■ *Pair work* Books closed. Put students in pairs, and give them 5–10 minutes to organize and write their stories. Make sure students understand that they are to include one mistake in the sequence of events in the story.

■ Have pairs form a small group with another pair and take turns reading their stories to each other and locating the mistakes.

■ Ask a few students to share their stories with the class, and have the class guess the mistake in each one.

Language close-up

9 WHAT DID THEY SAY?

This cloze activity has students complete the first part of Marie and Tom's conversation.

■ Books open. Have students fill in any blanks they can before watching the video.

■ Play this segment of the video through once, while students work alone to fill in the missing words and check their predictions.

■ Have students form pairs to compare answers, even if they are unsure of some, and then ask, "Does anyone need to watch this conversation again?" Rather than supplying answers, replay the segment as many times as necessary.

■ Check answers around the class by having selected students each read one of Tom's or Marie's lines.

■ Model the conversation or, if you wish, lead choral or individual repetition to prepare students for pair work. Then put the class into pairs to practice.

Answers

Marie: Hi. **There** will be **two** of us. . . .
Thank you. . . .

Tom: Marie! I'm really **sorry**. How **long** have you been waiting?

Marie: It's **OK**, Tom. I've only **been** here for a little **while**. Is everything all **right**?

Tom: Yes, it is **now**, but you won't **believe** what just happened to **me**.

Marie: Well, what **happened**?

Tom: Well, **first** of all, I was a little **late** leaving my **apartment**, and so I was in a **hurry**. Then, just after I **started** the car, I **remembered** I didn't have any **money** with me, so I went **back** to get my **wallet**.

Marie: Did you **find** it?

Tom: Oh, yes! I **found** it. That wasn't the **problem**. The problem **was** when I got **back** to my **car**, I couldn't **get** in.

Marie: Do you mean you **locked** your keys in the car?

Tom: That's **right**. So, guess what I did **after** that!

Marie: I **can't** guess.

Optional activity

Pair work Books open. Have pairs perform the conversation two more times. The first time, Marie should be very angry at Tom for being late. The second time, Tom should by very sorry and upset. (5 minutes)

🔟 *PRESENT PERFECT*

In these activities, students continue to work with the main verbs from the sequence, this time in present-perfect questions and answers with *Have you ever . . . ?*

A Books open. Explain the task, and ask a few students simple present-perfect questions such as "Have you ever arrived late for class?" to introduce the grammar point. (Note: It's not necessary to go into detail about the present perfect at this point.)

■ *Pair work* Have students work in pairs to complete the questions and then write three original present-perfect questions. As students work, circulate to check for accuracy.

Answers

1) Have you ever locked your keys in the car?
2) Have you ever called a lock service?
3) Have you ever left your wallet in the car?
4) Have you ever arrived late for an important dinner?
5) Have you ever gone to a restaurant without money?
6) Have you ever waited a long time for someone in a restaurant?

Additional sentences will vary.

B *Class activity* Books open. Have students stand and move about the classroom, asking these questions to at least three classmates. Ask students to mark a check next to a question every time someone answers "yes."

■ Bring students back together after about 5 minutes and ask, "Who got the most 'yes' answers to their questions?" and "Who do you think answered 'yes' to the most questions?"

■ Have selected students ask you their "best" original questions. Answer a student's question, and then ask that same question to another student, who answers, and then asks you one of his or her own questions.

11 Across the Golden Gate Bridge

Topics/functions: Asking and telling about places; giving advice

Structures: *Should* and *shouldn't*

Summary

In this sequence, Mr. and Mrs. Chang have just arrived at the San Francisco International Airport from Honolulu. They go directly to a car-rental agency in the airport. The car-rental agent at the counter greets them and asks if they have a reservation, which they do. He then asks them if they will be staying in San Francisco. Mrs. Chang tells him that they are going to visit friends in the Napa Valley, and the agent responds by mentioning the famous wineries and vineyards there. Then Mr. Chang asks him the best way to get to the Napa Valley, and Mrs. Chang asks if there is anything they should see along the way. The agent recommends that they cross the Golden Gate Bridge, stop in Sausalito, have lunch at Houlihan's restaurant, and visit Muir Woods, a redwood forest. As he describes the various places, they are shown in the sequence. The Changs thank the agent and leave to get the car. Suddenly, Mr. Chang realizes he doesn't have a map of the Napa Valley, but Mrs. Chang reassures him that they can get one in Sausalito. (Note: *The Napa Valley* is sometimes referred to as *Napa Valley* by local residents.)

 **Preview**

1 CULTURE

The culture preview in the Video Activity Book introduces essential information about the San Francisco area to build interest in and increase understanding of the sequence.

■ Books closed. On the board, write the following: Golden Gate Bridge, Napa Valley, Muir Woods, Sausalito. Ask the class, "Where are these places located?" If students are able to answer "California" or "near San Francisco," tell them

to open their books to the culture preview to learn more. If they are unable to answer, tell students to read the culture preview to find out where the places are located.

■ Books open. Have students read through the culture preview silently. Ask them to circle all of the place names they can find (e.g., San Francisco, Oakland Bay Bridge, San Francisco Bay, Berkeley, University of California, Golden Gate Bridge, Sausalito, Muir Woods, the Napa Valley).

■ Ask selected students to call out place names mentioned in the culture preview, and ask other students to say something about each place that is mentioned. For example:

A: Sausalito

B: A beautiful town on the water

■ Have students look at the map of the area, and say, "Imagine that you are a visitor to the San Francisco area. How could you get from one place to the next?" Ask selected students to respond. (Possible answers include rental car, bus, taxi, cable car, and train.)

■ Put students into pairs or small groups to work with the questions. Then ask several students to share their answers with the class.

2 VOCABULARY Taking a trip

In this activity, students are introduced to the names of places and sights presented in the video.

■ Books open. Have the class look carefully at each of the six pictures, and then explain the task.

■ *Pair work* Have students work in pairs to complete the task, and then have two pairs form a small group to compare answers.

■ Review the answers with the class.

Answers

1) winery	3) waterfront	5) forest
2) valley	4) bay	6) vineyard

3 *GUESS THE STORY*

In this activity, students use visual information in addition to what they have learned in the culture preview to predict where the Changs go first.

■ Books open. Ask students to first look at the three photos and then to look again at the map in the culture preview on page 48. Say, "If you were driving from San Francisco, which of these three places would you visit first? Mark an ✗ next to the photo of that place, and then compare your choice with a partner."

■ Tell students, "Now we will watch the sequence without the sound. Where do you think the couple goes first? Mark that place with a check."

■ Play the sequence with the sound off, while students watch and complete the task.

■ After students compare answers with a partner, tell them that the correct answer will become clear as they work with the video sequence. (Although the sequence does not actually show the Changs in Sausalito, it is clear that they plan to go there. At the end of the sequence, Mr. Chang says that he forgot to get a map of the Napa Valley, and Mrs. Chang tells him that they can get one after they have lunch in Sausalito.)

Optional activities

A Books closed. Write the questions below on the board, and review them with students. For your reference, the answers are given in parentheses.
1) How long do the Changs have for their trip? (one week)
2) Have they ever been to the area before? (no)
3) How will they get from place to place? (by rental car)
Have students watch the sequence again without the sound and predict the answers to these questions in writing as they watch. (5 minutes)

B *Pair work* Books closed. Play the beginning of the sequence again without the sound, and have pairs write a short dialogue to show what they think Ken and Mr. Chang first say to each other. Provide students with the following example:
Ken: Hello. May I help you?
Mr. Chang: Yes. I want to rent a car.

■ Have several pairs share their work with the class. Then play the beginning of the video with

the sound so that students can hear what Ken and Mr. Chang really do say. (10 minutes)

 *Watch the video*

4 *GET THE PICTURE*

In this activity, students watch and listen for the place names that the car-rental agent talks about.

■ Books open. Explain the task, and lead students through the list of place names.

■ Play the sequence through with the sound on. As they watch, have students circle the place names that they hear.

■ Have students compare answers with a partner. Replay the sequence if necessary, and then check answers around the class.

Answers

The Napa Valley	Muir Woods
Sausalito	The Golden Gate Bridge

Here is an alternative procedure for this activity:

■ Follow the procedure outlined above, but play the sequence through the first time with the sound on and the picture off. Ask students to listen and complete the task. Then have students check answers in pairs while watching the sequence with both the sound and picture on. (5 minutes)

5 *WATCH FOR DETAILS*

In this activity, students watch and listen for the reasons Ken gives the Changs for why they should visit certain places.

■ Books open. Explain the task, and lead students through the four photos by holding up your book, pointing to a photo and saying, "What is this a photo of?" [1) the Napa Valley, 2) Sausalito, 3) Houlihan's, 4) Muir Woods].

■ Play the entire sequence, and have students work alone to fill in the missing information as they watch.

■ Replay the sequence if needed before having students compare answers with their neighbors.

(procedure continues on next page)

Answers
1) The wineries and vineyards there are some of the most famous in California.
2) It's a fascinating little town just across the bridge.
3) It's right on the waterfront, and there's a wonderful view of San Francisco across the bay.
4) It's a beautiful redwood forest.

6 COMPLETE THE STORY

In this activity, students focus more closely on details in the sequence in order to complete a summary of the story.

■ Books open. Explain the task, and have students complete the paragraph before comparing answers with a partner.

■ Play the entire sequence so that students can check their answers and make any necessary changes.

■ Check answers around the class by having selected students each read aloud a sentence from the summary.

Answers
The Changs arrive in San Francisco from **Honolulu**. They **rent** a car at the airport for one **week** because they plan to visit friends in **the Napa Valley**. The rental agent tells them about the famous **wineries** there. They decide to drive across the **Golden Gate** Bridge and have lunch in **Sausalito** on the way.

Optional activity

Pair work Books closed. Have pairs take turns telling each other the events described in the paragraph, one line at a time. Tell them that their words need not be exact, but the events must be correct and in the proper order. Also, if either student makes a mistake, the pair must start over from the beginning. (10 minutes)

Follow-up

7 SAN FRANCISCO

In this activity, students synthesize information they have learned about San Francisco in this unit and in Unit 7 to plan a two-day visit to the area.

■ Books open. Explain the task, and lead students through the photos of famous San Francisco–area sights.

■ ***Group work*** Put students in small groups to plan their itineraries.

■ After 5–10 minutes, bring the class back together, and have each group describe their plans to the rest of the class.

Optional activities

After the groups have decided on their itineraries, you may want to add the following considerations and have groups plan their itineraries again.

A The group has an extremely limited amount of money to spend on the trip (e.g., US $100) and has to decide which activities they will cut from their plan. (5 minutes)

B The group now has just a single afternoon to spend in San Francisco and has to revise their itinerary accordingly. (5 minutes)

8 YOUR CITY

In these activities, students have the opportunity to talk more about places and give suggestions, as they plan an itinerary for the Changs' visit to their city.

A Books open. Explain the task, and model the sample language.

■ ***Group work*** Ask groups to discuss at least six suggestions for the Changs' visit.

B ***Class activity*** Books open or closed. Have each group share their itineraries with the class.

Language close-up

9 *WHAT DID THEY SAY?*

In this cloze activity, students complete the first part of the conversation between Ken, the car-rental agent, and the Changs.

■ Books open. Have students, working individually or in pairs, fill in any blanks they can before watching the video.

■ Play this section of the video as many times as necessary while students work alone to fill in the blanks and check their predictions.

■ Have students compare answers with a partner and then watch the video again to check their answers.

■ Model the conversation or, if you wish, lead a choral or individual repetition to prepare for pair work. Then have students form pairs to practice the dialogue between Ken and Mr. and Mrs. Chang.

Answers

Ken:	Good **morning**. May I **help** you?
Mr. Chang:	Yes, we're **here** to pick up a **car**.
Ken:	Do you **have** a reservation?
Mr. Chang:	Yes. The **name** is Chang.
Ken:	OK, Chang, Chang. Here it is, Mr. Chang. **Paid** in advance. **Sign** here and here. And that's for one **week** then?
Mr. Chang:	That's **right**. One week.
Ken:	Are you **staying** in San Francisco?
Mrs. Chang:	No, we're **going** to visit **friends** in the Napa Valley.
Ken:	Oh, Napa Valley. That's one of my **favorite** places. The wineries and **vineyards** there are some of the most **famous** in California.

Optional activity

Pair work Books open. Have pairs substitute their own information, including name, city, and sights in the local area, as they practice the conversation a second time. (5 minutes)

10 SHOULD *AND* SHOULDN'T
Giving advice

In these extension activities, students work with the modal *should* and the negative form *shouldn't* to give advice to people visiting their city.

A Books open. Explain the task, and then have students work alone to complete the sentences.

■ Have students compare their answers with a partner. Then check answers around the class by having selected students read the sentences aloud.

Answers
1) When you visit a foreign country, you should learn a few words of the local language.
2) You should find out about the weather before you travel.
3) You shouldn't carry a lot of cash when you travel.
4) You should talk to a travel agent about interesting places to visit.
5) You shouldn't be afraid to ask local people questions.

B *Pair work* Books open. Explain the task, and give pairs 5 minutes to complete the chart. Then have two pairs form a small group to compare answers.

■ Ask pairs to call out their answers, and create a class list on the board of things visitors should and shouldn't do.

Optional activities

A *Group work* Books closed. Have students work in small groups to list five things visitors to their school or to their classroom should or shouldn't do. (5 minutes)

B *Group work* Books closed. If time permits, have groups create posters that illustrate their suggestions for classroom or school visitors. (20 minutes)

12 Feeling bad

Topics/functions: Giving advice; talking about health problems

Structures: Modal verbs *may* and *could* for requests; suggestions

Summary

The sequence opens with Steve Clarke sitting at his office desk, which is covered with various cold medicines. It is clear that he has a terrible cold. Steve is checking his temperature when his co-worker Sandy comes up and gives him a cold remedy that she got at a health-food store. Next, Jim, another co-worker, stops by Steve's desk and tells him to try drinking the garlic juice his mother made; Jim leaves a large bottle of it with Steve. Then Rebecca enters and tells Steve that he can get rid of all his cold medicines because she knows the best remedy. She tells Steve that she would like to take him to lunch at a place where he can get "the best chicken soup in the world." Steve agrees, and says that he'll meet Rebecca downstairs. Steve starts to put all of the remedies in his briefcase, but changes his mind and sweeps them all into the wastebasket. The sequence ends with a happier-looking Steve leaving the office.

 **Preview**

1 CULTURE

The culture preview in the Video Activity Book introduces the topic of health care in the United States and Canada, and presents some key vocabulary used in the video.

■ Books open. Have students read the information in the culture preview silently and, as they read, circle the items that can be bought at drugstores and health-food stores (e.g., over-the-counter drugs, vitamins, natural foods).

■ Ask selected students to call out the answers. Then ask students if they think people in their country spend more or less on health care than people from the United States and Canada. Solicit answers around the class.

■ Have students stand up and walk around the classroom, asking the questions to various classmates. After a few minutes, bring the class back together and ask several students to share their answers.

2 VOCABULARY Cold remedies

In this activity, students classify according to type the various cold remedies and medications presented in the sequence.

■ *Pair work* Books open. Explain the task, and then have pairs sort the remedies into the correct categories.

■ Check answers around the class, and then have each pair add two more items of their own to each category. Ask students to compare responses in small groups.

■ To extend this activity, have each pair tell the class which remedy from each category they think is the best one. List these on the board to form a class list.

Answers

Home remedies	Over-the-counter drugs
chicken soup	aspirin
garlic juice	cough medicine
ginseng tea	
tea with lemon	

Additional remedies

Home remedies	Over-the-counter drugs
warm lemon juice	cold tablets
honey	cough drops

Optional activity

■ *Pair work* Books open. Have students, working with their original partners, rank all the remedies listed from most to least effective for curing a cold.

■ Have pairs form small groups to compare the way they have ranked the remedies. Then have each group report to the class on which remedy they think is most effective and why. (5 minutes)

3 GUESS THE STORY

In this activity, students prepare to work with the language of the sequence by watching the sequence without the sound in order to answer two central questions about the story.

■ Books open. Have students look at the photo of Steve, and ask, "What do you think is wrong with the man?" Have a few students share their predictions with the class.

■ Explain the task, and lead students through the two questions.

■ Play the sequence with the sound off. Have students answer the questions and then compare their predictions with a partner or around the class.

■ Ask several students what they think is wrong with the man and what his co-workers give him (e.g., "He has a cold." "His co-workers give him medicine."). Accept all answers at this point. Explain that the answers will become clear as students continue to work with the sequence.

Optional activities

A Books open. Play the sequence with the sound off again, and have students check the cold remedies listed in the chart in Activity 2 that they see in the video. (5 minutes)

B *Pair work* Books open. Have pairs list three adjectives to describe the man sitting at the desk. (5 minutes)

Possible answers
sick, tired, pale, miserable, uncomfortable, ill

 Watch the video

4 GET THE PICTURE

In this activity, students watch and listen to the sequence to find out how Steve's co-workers try to help him.

■ Books open. Have the class look at the three photos, and ask selected students to describe them.

■ Explain the task, and read through the possibilities under each photo with the class. If you wish, have students work in pairs to predict the answers before watching.

■ Play the sequence through with the sound on. Have students complete the task as they watch.

■ Play the sequence again if necessary, and then have students compare answers with a partner or around the class.

Answers
1) Sandy offers Steve something from a health-food store.
2) Jim offers Steve something his mother makes for him.
3) Rebecca says Steve should go out to lunch.

5 WATCH FOR DETAILS

In this activity, students focus more closely on details in the story by watching and listening for information about the remedies Steve's co-workers offer him.

■ Books open. Explain the task, and read through the items with the class.

■ Play the video sequence, and have students check the correct answers as they watch.

■ Replay the sequence if needed, and then have students compare their answers with a partner. Check answers around the class.

Answers

1) Sandy says her remedy contains ginseng/ makes you sleepy.
2) Jim says his remedy is great for a cold/ has garlic, onions, and carrots in it.
3) Rebecca says her remedy is the best cure of all.

Optional activity

■ *Group work* Books closed. Divide the class into three groups: the Sandy group, the Jim group, and the Rebecca group. Tell the class, "Now we're going to watch the sequence again. Write down as much information as you can about the remedy your person offers Steve. Then compare answers with the other students in your group."

■ As you play the sequence through with the sound on, have students write down as much information as they can.

■ Have students compare answers around their group, and then ask each group to compile a master list on the board. (10 minutes)

Possible answers

Sandy: She bought it at the health-food store. Mix it with hot water. Drink it. It works. It makes you sleepy. Don't drive after you take it. It's strong medicine.

Jim: It's an orange liquid, made with garlic, onions, and carrots. It looks like it tastes bad. It smells bad. Drink one cup every two hours.

Rebecca: The best cure of all is chicken soup. It tastes good. Get it at a restaurant.

6 WHAT'S YOUR OPINION?

In this activity, students give opinions about the effectiveness of the remedies offered and about whether or not Steve should be at work.

■ *Pair work* Books open. Lead students through the questions, and then put them into pairs to answer the questions.

■ Bring the class back together, and have pairs share their answers.

Optional activity

■ *Group work* Books open. Have students form groups to write three additional questions to exchange with another group.

■ Have groups exchange questions and then discuss and answer the questions. (10 minutes)

Possible questions

Does Jim really drink the garlic juice?
Why does Steve try so many medicines?
Why is Steve at work when he has a bad cold?
What's the worst cold remedy you know?

Follow-up

 Language close-up

7 HEALTH PROBLEMS

In these communicative activities, students suggest remedies for other ailments, role-play a conversation with Steve, and practice giving advice.

A Books open. Have students look at the four illustrations, and make sure they can pronounce the name of each ailment pictured. Have the students read each of the remedies listed.

■ *Group work* Explain the task. Then put students into groups to list two more remedies for each of the four problems.

■ Bring the class back together, and have the groups share their remedies for each problem. If you wish, have the class vote on the four best remedies.

Possible answers
1) a bad cold: Try some cold medicine. Drink orange juice.
2) a cough: It's important to take some cough medicine. Try some cough drops.
3) a headache: It's helpful to lie down. Drink a cup of coffee or tea. (Note: Caffeine, found in coffee and tea, relieves headaches.)
4) a backache: Get some backache cream. Put ice on your back.

B Books open. Explain the task, and model the sample conversation.

■ *Pair work* Have pairs take turns playing the roles of Steve and a co-worker who is offering him advice.

C Books open. Have students work in pairs to list two or three problems they would like to get advice on.

■ Have students change partners and then take turns asking for and giving advice, using their list of problems.

Optional activity

Group work Books open. Have groups invent one new or unusual remedy for each of the problems listed in Activity 1 (e.g., to cure a backache, sleep on a hard floor for three nights). (5 minutes)

8 WHAT DID THEY SAY?

This cloze activity has students complete the conversation between Sandy and Steve as they watch and listen to the video sequence.

■ Books open. Have students, working individually or in pairs, read through the conversation and fill in any blanks they can before watching.

■ Play the conversation between Sandy and Steve as many times as necessary. Have students work alone to check their predictions and fill in the blanks as they watch.

■ Have students compare answers in pairs. Then play the conversation again, and have students check their work.

■ Model the conversation or lead a choral and individual repetition to prepare students for pair work. Then put students into pairs to practice the conversation.

Answers
Sandy: How are those **papers** coming for this **afternoon**, Steve?
Steve: **Nearly** finished.
Sandy: Do you **still** have that **cold**?
Steve: Yeah, **it's** still pretty **bad**, Sandy.
Sandy: Listen, I've **got** just the **thing** for you. Just a **second**. . . . Here.
Steve: What's **that**?
Sandy: It's **something** I picked up at the **health**-food store. You just mix it with **hot** water and **drink** it.
Steve: But **what** is it?
Sandy: I'm not really **sure**. I think it **has** ginseng in it or something **like** that. Try it.
Steve: Are you sure it **works**?
Sandy: Of **course** it does.
Steve: Well, **thanks**, Sandy. That's really **nice**. Maybe later.

9 REQUESTS AND SUGGESTIONS

In these activities, students practice with *may* and *could* to make requests, and *should, try,* and *suggest* to give suggestions.

A Books open. Explain the task, and review the example. Then have students work alone to fill in the correct imperative forms of the verbs in the three conversations.

■ Have students compare answers with a partner, and then go over the answers with the class.

Answers

1) *At the office*
A: Here's the perfect cold medicine: garlic juice, onions, and carrots. You should drink a cup every two hours.
B: But I don't like carrots.
A: Well, then I suggest an old-fashioned bowl of chicken soup! And try to get some rest, too.

2) *At a pharmacy*
A: May I help you?
B: Yes. Could I have something good for a cold? It's a bad one.
A: Yes. I have these pills. They're a little strong. Just don't drive after you take them.
B: Hmm . . . I drive to work. Could I have something else?
A: Well, try these other pills then. They won't make you sleepy.

B Books open. Explain the task, making sure students understand that they should act out the conversation two times, the second time with different problems and remedies. Model the conversations with selected students.

■ *Pair work* Put students into pairs to practice, and then have several pairs act out their new conversations for the class.

Optional activity

■ *Pair work* Books closed. Have students work in pairs to come up with and describe a possible remedy for one of the following: baldness, tired eyes, sore feet, stiff shoulders.

■ Have each pair explain the "rules," using positive and negative imperatives, for taking or using this remedy.

■ Have students form new pairs, and then ask students to explain the problem chosen and the remedy suggested to their partner. (10 minutes)

Possible conversation
A: I've got a great remedy for tired eyes.
B: What is it?
A: Take a cloth. Wet it with hot water, and put it over your eyes. Don't open your eyes until the cloth cools. Try it.

At the Mall of America

 Preview

1 CULTURE

Shopping malls are very popular in the United States, and nearly every city has at least one. About 9 out of 10 people in the United States visit a shopping mall at least once a month. One out of eleven adults in the United States works at a shopping mall. The culture preview in the Video Activity Book introduces some information about the mall presented in the documentary – the Mall of America, the largest shopping and entertainment mall in the United States.

■ Books closed. Ask students, "Where do you usually go shopping?" Have a few selected students answer. Then ask, "Do you ever go to shopping malls?" Have students respond by raising their hands to indicate "yes" or "no." Then say, "Have you ever heard of the Mall of America? It's the biggest shopping mall in the United States. Open your books, and read about it in the culture preview."

■ Books open. Ask students to silently read through the culture preview. When they have finished, say, "Read the paragraph again and underline the facts that you found most interesting or surprising."

■ Ask several students to tell the class what items they underlined. Then read through the questions with the class, and put students into pairs or small groups to answer.

■ Ask several students to share their answers with the class.

Optional activity

■ **Pair work** Books closed. Ask students to work in pairs to predict five things they think one might find at the Mall of America.

■ Ask several pairs to share their predictions with the class, but be sure not to give away any answers at this point.

■ Tell students, "Now watch the documentary without sound. As you watch, check your predictions and list any other things you see." (10 minutes)

Watch the video

2 GET THE PICTURE

In this activity, students watch and listen in order to find five specific pieces of information about the Mall of America.

■ Books open. Explain the task, and read through the five items about the Mall of America with the class. Encourage students to predict the answers to any of the items if they feel confident doing so at this point.

■ Play the entire documentary with the sound on. Have students watch and check the correct answers as they view.

■ Have students compare answers with a partner. Then play the documentary again if necessary.

■ Go over the answers with the class by asking selected students to call out answers.

Answers
1) Bloomington, Minnesota.
2) hundreds of stores.
3) 14 cinemas.
4) 40 places to eat.
5) Camp Snoopy.

Optional activity

■ Books closed. Have students watch the documentary again and list any additional information they can about the mall (e.g., "There are four major department stores, dancing, music, and rides. There are visitors from several countries.").

■ Have students compare answers around class, and then compile a class list on the board. (5 minutes)

3 WATCH FOR DETAILS

In this activity, students watch and listen more closely in order to answer questions about what some of the people interviewed said they did at the mall.

■ Books open. Explain the task, and read through the information below each photo with the class.

■ Play the entire documentary. Have students check off the correct answers to the questions as they watch.

■ Have students compare answers in pairs. Then play the documentary again if necessary before going over the answers with the class.

Answers
1) She bought some shoes.
2) They went on rides./They looked in stores.
3) They bought some tapes.

---

4 WHAT THE SHOPPERS SAY

In this activity, students focus more closely on language by watching and listening in order to determine how three of the shoppers answered the reporter's questions.

■ Books open. Explain the task. Then have students read the three questions silently and predict the answers before viewing.

■ Play the sequence, and have students check and revise their predictions as they view.

■ Have students compare their answers with a partner before you go over them with the class.

Answers
1) Wear tennis shoes.
2) Come here if there's anything specific you're looking for.
3) Big. Real, real big.

Follow-up

5 WHAT'S YOUR OPINION?

In this activity, students have the opportunity to extend and personalize the information by giving their opinions about shopping malls and the Mall of America.

■ Books open. Explain the task, and read through the three questions with the class.

■ **Pair work** Put students into pairs to take turns asking and answering the questions.

■ Bring the class back together, and have pairs share their responses with the class.

Optional activity

■ **Group work** Books open. Have students work in small groups to write five additional questions about shopping and shopping malls. Then have two groups exchange questions.

Possible questions
How would you spend your time at the mall?
What kinds of stores would you look for at the mall?
What would you do when you first arrived at the mall?
Do you think the Mall of America is too big?
Do you like small stores or large malls?

■ Give the groups a few minutes to discuss the questions that they have received. Then have each group share their most interesting question and answer with the class. (10 minutes)

Topics/functions: Ordering food

Structures: *Would* and *will*

Summary

The video sequence shows a variety of the foods and activities at the Minnesota state fair. In the sequence, three short vignettes focus on some of the people at the fair. Steve and Liz buy corn on the cob from a vendor. Three friends, Rick, Betsy, and Nancy, win a large stuffed animal at a game and then order a meal at an outdoor restaurant. Cynthia and Paul go on a typical amusement park–style ride that spins and tilts, which leaves Paul feeling rather ill. After the ride, Cynthia says she is hungry, but Paul responds negatively. Still, when Cynthia sees an ice-cream stand she orders a cone with three scoops: one for her and two for Paul. Just as she thought, Paul feels well enough to eat some of the ice cream.

Preview

1 CULTURE

Each of the fifty states in the United States has a state fair in the summer, and many communities also have local fairs. The fairs are often organized around an agricultural theme. In New York State, there are corn and strawberry festivals. In West Virginia, there are fairs celebrating pumpkins and apples. The culture preview in the Video Activity Book introduces the topic of the sequence by presenting information about state fairs in the United States and Canada.

■ Books closed. Ask students, "Have you ever been to a fair or festival?" Have students raise their hands to indicate "yes." Then write the following categories on the board:
Things to Do
Things to Eat
Things to See

■ Have students work in pairs to list the things they *think* people can do, eat, and see at fairs in the United States and Canada.

■ Bring the class back together, and have pairs call out the things they have listed. Write these on the board to form a class list. (Note: Leave the list on the board as students will need to refer to it in upcoming activities.)

Possible answers

Things to Do
go on rides (e.g., merry-go-round or roller coaster), play games, win prizes, ride a horse, walk around

Things to Eat
hot dogs, hamburgers, ice cream, pie, doughnuts, corn on the cob, fruits (e.g., apples, strawberries, watermelon)

Things to See
farm animals (e.g., pigs, cows, sheep, horses), farm equipment (e.g., tractors), arts and crafts (e.g., furniture, baskets, paintings, pottery), homegrown fruits and vegetables (e.g., corn, pumpkins, squash, apples)

■ Books open. Have students silently read the culture preview to compare the items that they have listed with the information given.

■ Put students into pairs or small groups to work with the questions about fairs and family fun, and then have selected students share their answers with the class.

2 VOCABULARY At a state fair

In this activity, students are introduced to vocabulary related to the typical fair activities and foods presented in the sequence.

■ Books open. Ask students to look at the six illustrations and, if possible, describe what they see in each.

■ *Pair work* Have students work in pairs to match the illustrations with the names of activities, and then have students compare answers with another pair.

■ Go over the answers with the class, and explain to students that they will see all of these things in the video sequence.

Answers
1) win a prize
2) ride on a roller coaster
3) eat corn on the cob
4) ride a horse
5) ride on a merry-go-round
6) eat ice cream

Optional activities

A *Class activity* Books open. Have students walk around the classroom, asking each other "Have you ever" questions about the six activities pictured in the exercise (e.g., "Have you ever eaten corn on the cob?") and keeping a written record of the answers.

■ Bring the class back together after 5 minutes, and have selected students share their results with the class. (10 minutes)

B *Pair work* Books open. Ask students, working in pairs, to predict what other things they will see people doing at the fair in the video sequence. (Note: To help students make their predictions, have them review both the master class list of fair and festival activities written on the board and the culture preview.)

■ Have a few pairs share their predictions with the class, and accept all answers at this point.

■ Play the sequence through (if you feel appropriate, at a faster than normal speed) with the sound off, as students watch to check their predictions. (10 minutes)

3 GUESS THE STORY

In this activity, students prepare to watch the sequence by making predictions about the story based on visual information.

■ Books open. Ask students to look at the photos, and explain the task.

■ Have students work alone to make their predictions and then compare answers with a partner. Tell students that they will be able to check their predictions when they watch the video. (Betsy wins the prize.)

Optional activity

■ *Group work* Have students from the same cultural background form small groups. Play the sequence again without the sound, and have groups list the things they see that are also common at fairs and festivals in their cultures.

■ Have each group share their responses with the class. (5 minutes)

 Watch the video

4 GET THE PICTURE

In this activity, students watch and listen to the sequence to find out what people did at the fair.

■ Books open. Have students look at the three photos, and ask a few students to describe what they see in them.

■ Explain the task, and lead students through the list of activities.

■ Play the entire sequence with the sound on. As they watch, have students check off the things they see the person or people in the photos doing.

■ Have students compare their work with a partner. Then check answers around the class.

Answers
Liz and Steve
3) ate some corn on the cob (Steve)

Nancy, Betsy, and Rick
1) won a prize (Nancy)
5) had some lunch

Paul and Cynthia
2) had some ice cream
4) went on a ride

5 WATCH FOR DETAILS

In the first activity, students focus on detail in the sequence by watching and listening in order to make a complete list of all the things to do, eat, or see at the state fair. In the second activity, students have a chance to relate the material to their own lives by indicating which of these they have done, eaten, or seen.

A Books open. Explain the task, and lead students through the three categories.

■ Play the sequence through as many times as necessary. Have students work alone to list items as they watch.

■ Have students compare their lists in small groups. Then have students call out their answers. Write these on the board to form a class chart.

■ Play the sequence again so that students can check it against the class chart.

B Books open. Explain the task, and have students check off appropriate items on their lists. Then have students form pairs and compare.

Answers

Things to do	*Things to eat*	*Things to see*
ride a horse	corn on the cob	rodeo
play games	hot dogs	amusement
ride on a	french fries	rides
merry-go-	hamburgers	animals
round	ice cream	
ride on a		
roller coaster		

6 A DAY AT THE FAIR

In these communicative activities, students use information from the sequence to plan a day at the fair and then to role-play having lunch there.

A Books open. Have students look at the photos of scenes from the sequence, and then explain the task.

■ *Group work* Have students work together in groups of four or five to plan their day at the fair. Make sure students understand that all members of their group must agree on the five activities.

■ Bring the class back together, and have each group describe their day at the fair. Then have the class vote on which group has planned the "best" day.

B *Pair work* Books open. Have students form pairs, and explain that each student in the pair should take a turn being a waiter or waitress while the other orders food.

■ If you wish, have a few pairs act out their conversations for the class.

Optional activity

■ *Group work* Books closed. Have students work in groups of three to act out one of the three scenes in the sequence in which food is ordered. Tell the groups that they should decide which scene they will act out and stay as close as possible to the language and actions of the characters in that scene. (Note: The scene in which Nancy, Betsy, and Rick order food has four people. Advise groups that if they choose this scene, one student will have to take the role of more than one character. Alternatively, have some students work in groups of four, and assign them this scene.)

■ Play the entire sequence several times as students work on their scenes. Then give groups 5 minutes to practice.

■ Have groups who have chosen the same scene perform for each other. (15 minutes)

7 YOUR COUNTRY

In these activities, students personalize the topic and share information with each other by listing and discussing the things they can eat, do, and see at fairs in their own countries.

A Group work Books open. Explain the task, and have students from the same culture form small groups to list the things they can do, eat, and see at fairs in their country.

■ Bring the class back together, and have selected students from each group call out items from each column.

B Books open. Explain the task, and have students each check their favorite things in their lists.

■ Model the short conversation, and then tell students to walk around the class and have similar conversations with as many classmates as possible.

C Books closed. Explain the task, and have students form random small groups to discuss popular foods in their cultures and in the cultures of other group members.

■ Have a few students share their answers with the class.

Optional activity

■ *Pair work* Books open or closed. Have students from the same culture work in pairs to write a brief description of a popular festival food from their country that is similar to food seen in the sequence. For example, Japanese students might write, "Tomorokoshi is roasted corn. It's not served with butter. It's served with soy sauce."

■ Have pairs read their descriptions to the class. (10 minutes)

 Language close-up

8 WHAT DID THEY SAY?

This cloze activity has students watch and listen to complete the conversation in which Steve and Liz buy corn, and the conversation in which the three friends, Nancy, Rick, and Betsy, order food.

■ Books open. Have students, working individually or in pairs, fill in any blanks they can in the first conversation, (1), before watching the sequence.

■ Play the appropriate scene in the sequence through as many times as necessary while students work alone to check their predictions and fill in the blanks.

■ Have students compare answers with a partner and then watch the scene again as a final check.

■ Repeat these steps with conversation (b). Then go over the answers with the class.

■ Model the first conversation, and put students into groups of three to practice. Have groups practice three times so that each student has a chance to play each of the three characters.

■ Model the second conversation, and have groups of four practice. Remind groups to practice the conversation four times, switching roles each time.

Answers
1) Vendor: Hey, this is the **place**! Get your fresh corn on the **cob** here! Fresh, **hot**-roasted **corn** on the cob! . . . What **would** you like?
   Steve: I'll **have** one of **those**, please.
   Vendor: Coming **up**. . . . What about **you**? Would you **like** one, too?
   Liz: Not right **now**, thank you. I'm not **hungry**.
   Steve: Maybe you **should** give us another **one** anyway!
   Vendor: Sure.

2) Nancy: Oh, he is *so* **cute**!
   Rick: Yeah, but that **was** a lot of **work**.
   Now let's **find** a place to **eat**.
   Betsy: How about over **there**? There's a **restaurant** where we can **sit** down, too. My **feet** are tired. . . .
   Waitress: Hi! **May** I take your **order**?
   Betsy: Yeah, I **think** I'll have a hot **dog** and a small **order** of french fries.
   Waitress: Would you **like** anything to **drink**?
   Betsy: I'll have a **small** diet cola.
   Waitress: OK. And **what** can I **get** for you?
   Nancy: I guess **I'd** like the **salad** plate and a cup of **tea**, please.

Optional activity

▪ *Group work* Books closed. Put students into groups of three. Then play the scene in which Paul and Cynthia buy an ice-cream cone from the vendor.

▪ Have each student in a group take a different character in this scene and then write out that character's lines. Play the scene several times as students work on their lines.

▪ Check the lines against the transcript, and have students practice acting out the conversation. (10 minutes)

9 WOULD *AND* WILL
Ordering food

In these activities, students practice ordering food – the functional focus of the sequence – using sentences with *would* and *will* – the grammatical focus of the sequence.

A Books open. Explain the task, and model the example sentence. Make sure students understand that the expression, "*Would you like* . . . ?" means the same thing as the expression, "*Do you want* . . . ?" but is more polite.

▪ Have students work alone to complete the task and then compare answers with a partner as you circulate and check for accuracy.

▪ Review the answers with the class.

Answers
1) What would you like to eat?
2) Would you like french fries or a baked potato with that?
3) Would you like dessert?
4) Would you like anything to drink?

B *Pair work* Books open. Explain the task, and review the example. Then put students into pairs to take turns ordering a meal.

▪ If you wish, have several pairs act out their role plays for the class.

14 Around the World: the game show

Topics/functions: Asking and answering
questions about geography

Structures: Comparisons with adjectives

Summary

The sequence opens with an announcer
introducing the TV game show "Around the
World." We then see the game-show set; the host,
Johnny Traveler; and three contestants. On the
wall in large letters are the game-show question
categories: Rivers and Waterfalls, Deserts and
Mountains, Cities and Countries, and Oceans and
Islands. The announcer introduces the three
contestants: Marlene Miller, a computer engineer
from Seattle; Jack Richardson, a high school
teacher from Boston; and Kathy Hernandez, an
accountant from Vero Beach, Florida. As the
game show progresses, all three contestants do
fairly well, but at the end of the game Marlene
has the most points. However, she is disappointed
with her prize, two plane tickets to Seattle,
Washington. Marlene lives in Seattle.

 *Preview*

1 CULTURE

TV game shows in the United States and Canada
are very popular, and regular viewers almost
never miss an episode of long-running shows like
Jeopardy (a general-knowledge quiz show), which
is shown every weeknight. The culture preview in
the Video Activity Book introduces the topic of
TV game shows in the United States and Canada
and presents some information about various
popular shows.

■ Books closed. Ask the class, "Do you ever watch
game shows on television?" Have students raise
their hands to indicate "yes."

■ Write the names of the game shows listed in the
box on the right in the culture preview on the
board, and say "These are popular game shows in

the United States and Canada. What kind of
game show do you think each one is? Do you
think it is easy or hard?"

■ Put students into small groups to make
predictions, and then check predictions around
the class.

■ Books open. Have students check their
predictions against the information in the box in
the culture preview. Then say, "Do game-show
players have to be smart? Read the information in
the culture preview silently to find out."

■ Check the answer (No, sometimes winners are
just lucky.), and then put students into small
groups to work with the questions.

■ Have various students share their answers with
the class.

Optional activity

Group work Books closed. Have students from
similar cultural backgrounds form small groups
and list what they think are the three most
popular game shows in their countries. Have each
group then choose one of the shows and explain
to the class how it is played and what kinds of
prizes winners receive. (10 minutes)

2 GUESS THE FACTS

In this activity, students become familiar with the
format of the game show "Around the World" by
predicting answers to some of the questions they
will hear in the sequence.

■ Books closed. Ask students two or three questions
with comparatives about the area where your
school is located. Have selected students answer.

■ ***Pair work*** Books open. Say, "Now, we'll try to
answer six more questions about geography."
Explain the task, and lead students through the
questions. Then put students into pairs to answer
each one. (Note: Do not give the answers to the
students at this point. Tell them that they will have
a chance to check their answers later in the lesson.)

Optional activities

A Books closed. Play the entire sequence with the sound off, and then have students each choose one of the three contestants to describe.

■ On the board write the three names (Marlene, Jack, Kathy), and compile a class description of each person. (10 minutes)

Possible descriptions

Marlene
She's in her thirties. She has black hair and brown eyes. She's wearing a yellow dress.

Jack
He's in his late forties. He has blond hair that is beginning to turn gray. He's wearing a dark blue jacket, a blue shirt, and a red tie. He's tall.

Kathy
She's in her late thirties. She has straight brown hair and brown eyes. She's wearing a blue dress.

B Books closed. Play the entire sequence with the sound off, and then have students predict who the winner is and what prize he or she receives at the end of the sequence. (Note: Be sure not to give away the answer at this point.) (5 minutes)

 Watch the video

3 CHECK THE FACTS

In this activity, students watch and listen in order to check their predictions and, if necessary, correct their answers from Exercise 2.

■ Books open. Explain the task, and have students turn back to the beginning of Exercise 2 on page 62.

■ Play the entire sequence with the sound on, and have students check and correct their predictions while viewing.

■ Have students compare their work with a partner, and then check answers around the class.

Answers
1) the Nile River
2) Mt. McKinley
3) Australia
4) the Gobi Desert
5) Mexico City
6) Venezuela

4 WATCH FOR DETAILS

In this activity, students focus more closely on details in the story by watching and listening for personal information about Marlene, Jack, and Kathy.

■ Books open. Have students look at the three photos, and then explain the task.

■ Read through the six exercise items with the students, and encourage them to check any answers they think they know.

■ Play the entire sequence with the sound on. Have students answer the questions as they watch and then compare answers with a partner.

■ Replay the sequence if needed, and then go over the answers with the class.

Answers
1) Seattle, Washington.
2) computer engineer.
3) Boston, Massachusetts.
4) high school teacher.
5) Vero Beach, Florida.
6) accountant.

5 WHO WINS THE GAME?

In these activities, students reinforce their understanding of details in the sequence by watching and listening to find out each contestant's score and whether or not the winner is happy with the prize.

A Books open. Explain the task. Then play the entire sequence with the sound on. Have students, working individually, complete the task by writing what each person's score is at the end of the game.

■ Ask students to compare answers with a partner. Then play the sequence again if necessary before going over the answers with the class.

Answers
Marlene   250
Jack   150
Kathy   50

(procedure continues on next page)

B Books open. Read the questions with the class, and then have students discuss them in pairs or small groups.

■ Have various students share their answers with the class.

Answer

Marlene is not happy about winning a trip to Seattle because she lives in Seattle.

Optional activities

A Books closed. Have students watch the end of the sequence again and list the things they see and hear that indicate Marlene is unhappy with her prize (e.g., her facial expression, her tone of voice, the sudden end of the show). (5 minutes)

B *Pair work* Books closed. Have students work in pairs to write what they think Marlene is saying to Jack as the theme music comes up at the end of the sequence. (5 minutes)

Possible answer

Marlene: I can't believe it! What a terrible prize! . . . I know! I'll explain to Johnny that I live in Seattle. Maybe I can go somewhere else. . . .

Follow-up

6 AROUND THE WORLD

Students further develop their comprehension by writing comparative questions and using them to play their own version of the game "Around the World."

A *Group work* Books open. Explain the task, and then put students into groups of four or five to write game-show questions similar to those asked in the video. Emphasize to students that they must know the answers to any questions that they write. Circulate to help and check for accuracy. [Note: If students don't like the categories suggested, they may choose categories of their own (e.g., sports, music). New categories should be chosen and agreed upon by the class.]

B *Class activity* Books open. After 5–10 minutes, bring the class back together to play the game "Around the World." Explain the procedure, and model the sample language with a volunteer.

■ Have the small groups join together to form two groups, Group A and Group B, to play a round of the game. Group A chooses a game-show host to ask questions. Members of Group B take turns choosing categories and answering questions. Play the game for about 5 minutes.

■ Have the groups switch roles and play the game for another 5 minutes.

Optional activities

A Books open. Have students work alone to rank the categories in order of personal difficulty, and then have pairs compare responses. Select several students to share their rankings with the class. (5 minutes)

B *Group work* Books open. Have students work in small groups to write what they consider to be one or two difficult questions for each category. Then have each group choose a player. Ask these players to come to the front of the room, choose categories, and answer the various groups' questions. The student who answers the most questions correctly becomes the class champion. (10 minutes)

Language close-up

7 WHAT DID THEY SAY?

This cloze activity has students watch and listen to complete the dialogue of the announcer and the host, Johnny Traveler, at the beginning of the sequence.

■ Books open. Have students work individually or in pairs to read through the dialogue and fill in any blanks they can before watching.

■ Play this segment of the sequence as many times as needed. Have students check their predictions and fill in the blanks as they watch.

■ Have students check their answers with a partner. Then play this segment of the sequence again so that students can check their answers against the video.

■ Go over answers with the class.

■ Model the dialogue or lead a choral repetition to prepare for pair work. Then put students into pairs to practice.

Answers

Announcer: And now it's **time** to play "Around the **World**" with your host Johnny Traveler.

Johnny: **Ladies** and gentlemen, **welcome** to "Around the World," the **game** show about world **geography**. And now, let's **meet** our players.

Announcer: A **computer** engineer from **Seattle**, Washington, Marlene Miller! A high **school** teacher from **Boston**, Massachusetts, Jack Richardson! And from Vero Beach, Florida, an **accountant**, Kathy Hernandez!

Johnny: **Welcome** to "Around the World." And now, let's **begin** our game. Our categories are **Deserts** and Mountains, **Rivers** and Waterfalls, Oceans and **Islands**, Cities and **Countries**. Marlene, please begin.

Optional activity

Pair work Books open. Have pairs practice and perform the dialogue in their best announcer and game-show host voices, substituting the names and occupations of three classmates in place of Marlene, Jack, and Kathy. (5 minutes)

8 COMPARISONS WITH ADJECTIVES

In these activities, students practice writing, asking, and answering comparative questions and answers, the grammatical focus of the sequence.

A Books open. Explain the task, and model the example. (Note: It is not necessary to provide a complete grammatical analysis of comparatives at this point.) Point out to students that they need to use the superlative form of the adjective when comparing more than two items.

■ Have students work alone to write the questions for items (2) through (5). Then have students compare their work with a partner. Circulate to

check for problems, and then go over the questions with the class.

■ Now have students, working individually, write three questions of their own. Encourage students to write questions for which they know the answers.

■ As students work, circulate to help and check for accuracy.

B *Pair work* Books open. When most students seem finished, have them form pairs and take turns asking and answering each other's questions. For your reference, answers are given in parentheses.

Answers

1) Which city is colder, New York or Tokyo? (New York is colder.)
2) Which planet is the biggest, Earth, Saturn, or Mars? (Saturn is the biggest.)
3) Which plane is faster, the Concorde or a 747? (The Concorde is faster.)
4) Which building is older, the World Trade Center or the Empire State Building? (The Empire State Building is older.)
5) Which country is the largest, Brazil, Canada, or Argentina? (Canada is the largest.)

Optional activities

A *Pair work* Books open. Have students form new pairs to play another round of "Around the World." (5 minutes)

B *Pair work* Books closed. Have students work in pairs to write three additional comparative questions and answers about the city they are in or the school where they are studying, and then share these with the class in a game format. (10 minutes)

C Books open or closed. Have students work alone to write three comparative questions about Marlene, Jack, and Kathy, and then take turns asking and answering questions with a partner. (5 minutes)

Possible questions
Who is taller, Jack or Marlene?
Who is smarter, Marlene or Jack?

15 May I speak to Cathy?

Topics/functions: Making a telephone call; giving and receiving messages

Structures: Requests with *tell* and *ask*

Summary

As the sequence opens, John Waite is preparing to paint his living room ceiling. Just as he climbs up the ladder, the phone rings, so he has to climb down to answer it. The phone call is for his daughter, Cathy, and since she is not home, John takes a message. This happens two more times, and each time, John takes a message. When Cathy gets home, she asks her father if there were any calls. He tells her who called and that the messages are next to the phone. Cathy goes to get her messages, and John starts painting again. When the phone rings, John starts to get down off the ladder to answer it, but Cathy calls out that she will get it. Relieved, he goes back to work. This time, though, it is John's boss who is calling. As Cathy holds the phone and waits for her father to come and take the call, she hears a loud crash from the living room. Concerned, she calls out "What happened?" to her father. John replies that he is OK, but when he comes into the kitchen to take the phone, he is covered with paint. Though upset, he tells his boss that there is "No problem at all."

 **Preview**

1 CULTURE

In the United States and Canada, local telephone calls from pay phones cost about 25 cents. For this price, people can talk for 5 minutes. In their homes, people usually pay a fixed monthly rate that allows them to make unlimited local calls. On average, each person in the United States and Canada makes about 3,500 calls per year. The average call lasts about 7 minutes. Seventy percent of U.S. and Canadian households have two or more phones, and 46 percent have answering machines. Many households pay an additional fee for extra services such as call waiting or call forwarding. The culture preview in the Video Activity Book prepares students to work with the sequence by describing these extra services.

■ Books closed. Ask the class, "Who likes to talk on the phone?" Have students respond by raising their hands to indicate that they do.

■ Ask, "Who has an answering machine?" Again, have students respond by raising their hands.

■ On the board, write the following:
Call waiting   Call forwarding

■ Have students work in pairs to guess what these things are and then write out their predictions.

■ Books open. Have students read the information in the culture preview silently to check and, if necessary, revise their predictions.

■ Have students work with the questions in pairs or small groups. When talk begins to die down, bring the class back together to share their answers.

Optional activity

Books closed. Have students work in pairs or small groups to list the ways in which their lives would be different if they did not have telephones. Then have various students share their lists with the class. (5 minutes)

Possible answers

I couldn't talk to my friends or relatives as often as I do.

It would be more difficult to make plans with friends.

It would be more difficult to get information (e.g., movie or train schedules).

I wouldn't have expensive phone bills.

I would write more letters.

I would be able to study without interruptions.

2 VOCABULARY *Telephone expressions*

In these activities, students work with common expressions for giving and receiving messages that are used in the sequence and then have an opportunity to think of additional expressions that can be used.

A Books open. Explain the task, and read through the list of telephone expressions [items (1) through (8)] with the class.

■ *Pair work* Have students work in pairs to match the telephone expressions with the appropriate language function.

■ Have pairs compare answers around the class before you go over them.

Answers
1) c   5) b
2) a   6) d
3) c   7) a
4) d   8) b

B *Pair work* Books open. Have pairs list three additional telephone expressions and then compare answers with another pair.

■ Ask various students to share their answers, and write these on the board.

Possible additional telephone expressions
Is Cathy there?
She's busy right now.
She can't come to the phone just now.
Could you ask her to call me?
Are you expecting her soon?

3 GUESS THE STORY

In this activity, students prepare to work with the language of the sequence by watching to predict the expressions used to begin two of the telephone conversations.

■ Books open. Explain the task, and have students look at the photos. Ask, "What do you think these people are saying?"

■ Have students, working individually or in pairs, choose appropriate expressions from Exercise 2 to write in each of the speech balloons.

■ Play the first two minutes of the sequence without the sound. Have students check and revise their predictions as they watch.

■ Have students compare their answers with a partner, and then have several pairs share their predictions with the class. Accept all reasonable answers.

Optional activity

Play the entire sequence with the sound off, and have students do one of the following: count the number of phone calls made, write three adjectives to describe how they think John feels each time he has to come down off the ladder, describe John, describe the house, or say why John is at home and not at work. (5 minutes)

Possible answers
Number of phone calls: four
Adjectives to describe how John feels: frustrated, annoyed, tired, angry
Description of John: He's in his late forties or early fifties. He's tall and has brown hair and eyes. He's wearing blue jeans and a plaid shirt.
Why John is at home: He's on vacation. He took a day off to paint the living room. It's Saturday.

Watch the video

4 GET THE PICTURE

In these activities, students watch and listen to decide on the correct order of the callers and to say whether each caller will call back or instead wants Cathy to return the call.

A Books open. Explain the task, and have students look at the photos.

■ Play the entire sequence with the sound on, and have students work alone to number the calls in the order in which they occur.

■ Have students compare their answers with a partner. Then go over the answers with the class.

Answers
1) Kevin
2) Jenny
3) Rachel

B Books open. Explain the task. Then play the entire sequence with the sound on again. Have students work alone to complete each telephone message for Cathy by writing the name of the caller and checking the correct message.

■ Have students compare their choices with a partner. Then go over the answers with the class.

Answers
1) Kevin called. He wants Cathy to call.
2) Jenny called. She will call Cathy back.
3) Rachel called. She wants Cathy to call.

5 TELEPHONE ETIQUETTE

These activities reinforce students' understanding of the language used in the sequence by having them watch and listen to determine what each caller says and which one is the most polite.

A Books open. Explain the task by reading the instructions with the class.

■ Play the entire sequence with the sound on once or twice. As they watch, have students write what Kevin, Jenny, and Rachel each say to Cathy's father when he answers the phone.

■ Have students compare answers with a partner. Then play the conversations again, and have students check their work.

■ Review the answers with the class.

Answers
1) Kevin: Hello, may I speak to Cathy?
2) Jenny: Hello, Mr. Waite. This is Jenny. Is Cathy home?
3) Rachel: Hi. This is Rachel. Is Cathy home?

B *Pair work* Explain the task, and then put students into pairs to discuss which of the three callers they think is the most polite. Encourage them to try to explain why one person is more polite than another.

■ Bring the class back together, and have pairs share their answers and reasons with the class.

Answer
Jenny is the most polite because she gives her name and greets Mr. Waite by name when he answers the phone.

Optional activities

A Books open. Have students rank the three callers from most to least polite. (While they are all polite, Jenny is the most polite, followed by Rachel, and then Kevin.) (5 minutes)

B Books open. Have students use Jenny's dialogue as a model in rewriting Kevin's and Rachel's lines so that they are just as polite. (5 minutes)

Possible answers
Kevin: Hello, Mr. Waite. This is Cathy's friend Kevin. May I speak to her?
Rachel: Hello, Mr. Waite. This is Rachel. Is Cathy home?

6 WHAT'S YOUR OPINION?

In this activity, students decide which of the telephone conveniences (described in the culture preview) Mr. Waite needs.

■ *Pair work* Books open. Explain the task. Then have students, working in pairs, rank the telephone conveniences listed in the culture preview from most to least useful for Mr. Waite. Encourage students to give reasons for their choices.

■ Bring the class back together, and have various pairs share their ideas.

Possible answer
Mr. Waite needs an answering machine and two telephone lines on one phone so that he can tell who each call is for. He needs call forwarding, too. Then Cathy could have received her calls at the place where she was that afternoon.

 Follow-up

7 FINISH THE STORY

These extension activities further develop students' understanding of telephone conversations and etiquette by having them write and then act out possible phone conversations between Mr. Waite and his boss.

A *Pair work* Books open. Explain the task, and have students look at the photos. Then model the beginning of the conversation between Mr. Waite and his boss, and put students into pairs to write an ending for it. Encourage students to be creative.

■ Give pairs between 5–10 minutes to finish the conversation. As students work, circulate to help with vocabulary. When time is up, give students a few minutes to practice their conversations.

B Books open. Have each pair act out their conversation for the class. (Note: In large classes, this activity can be done in groups.)

■ If you wish, have the class (or the groups) vote on the funniest, the most realistic, and the most dramatic conversations.

 Language close-up

8 WHAT DID THEY SAY?

This cloze exercise has students watch and listen to fill in missing words in the conversations between Mr. Waite and the three friends who call Cathy.

■ Books open. Explain the task, and have students work alone or in pairs to read through the conversations and fill in any blanks they can before watching.

■ Play this segment of the sequence with the sound on. Have students check their predictions and complete the conversations as they watch.

■ Have students compare answers, and replay any or all of the conversations as necessary.

■ Go over the answers with the class, and then replay this segment of the sequence so that students can hear the answers in context.

■ Model the conversations, and then put students into pairs to practice. If you wish, have selected pairs act out one of the conversations for the class.

Answers
1) Mr. Waite: Hello?
   Kevin: Hello, **may** I speak **to** Cathy?
   Mr. Waite: I'm **sorry**. She's not **in** just now.
   Kevin: Is she **coming** back soon?
   Mr. Waite: Uh, **yes**, I think **so**.
   Kevin: Well, **could** you tell **her** that Kevin **called** and that I'll call **back** later?
   Mr. Waite: **Sure**, Kevin.
   Kevin: **Thank** you. Good-bye.
   Mr. Waite: Bye.

(answers continue on next page)

2) Mr. Waite: Hello?
   Jenny: **Hello**, Mr. Waite. **This** is Jenny. Is Cathy **home**?
   Mr. Waite: Oh, hi, Jenny. No, Cathy's **not** here right **now**.
   Jenny: **Will** she be **back** soon?
   Mr. Waite: Uh, I'm not **sure**. Would you **like** to leave a **message**?
   Jenny: Well, **could** you just **tell** her to call **me** when she **comes** in?
   Mr. Waite: Sure, **I'll** tell her. **Bye**, Jenny.
   Jenny: Bye, **Mr.** Waite.

3) Mr. Waite: Hello?
   Rachel: **Hi**, this is Rachel. **Is** Cathy home?
   Mr. Waite: Uh, no, she's **not**, Rachel. **Would** you like her to **call** you **when** she comes **in**?
   Rachel: Yes, **please**. She has my **number**.
   Mr. Waite: I'll **tell** her, Rachel. Bye.
   Rachel   Bye.

Optional activity

Books closed. Play the segment of the sequence in which Cathy answers the phone. Have students work alone to write down exactly what she says when she answers the phone and then compare with a partner. (Cathy says, "Hello? Uh, no, actually, he's busy right now. Oh, OK. I'll call him then.") (5 minutes)

9 REQUESTS WITH TELL AND ASK

In this activity, students personalize the topic by using their own information in making requests with *tell* and *ask*, the structural focus of the unit.

■ Books open. Explain the task, and model the two requests given as examples. (Note: At this point, it is not necessary to provide a detailed grammatical analysis of how requests are made in English.)

■ *Pair work* Explain the task, and put students into pairs to practice the conversations in Exercise 8, adapting them with their own information. If time permits, have students change partners once or twice.

■ Bring the class back together, and have several pairs each act out one of the conversations for the class.

Optional activities

A *Pair work* Books open or closed. Have students work in pairs to write a telephone conversation between Cathy and Mr. Waite's boss for the following situation: Mr. Waite is not home, and his boss wants to talk to him as soon as he returns. Tell students to write the conversation so that both speakers are very polite. (10 minutes)

B *Group work* Books closed. In groups of three, have students follow this procedure: Student A requests something of student C – with student B relaying the request. Student C then gives a reason why she/he cannot comply with the request and tells this to student B. Then student B relays this information to student A. Have students take a turn playing each role. (10 minutes)

Possible dialogue

A (to B): Would you ask Tomoko to pass me the eraser?
B (to C): Would you please pass the eraser to Jin Sook?
C (to B): Please tell Jin Sook that I don't have the eraser.
B (to A): Tomoko says that she doesn't have the eraser.

16 A whole new Marty

Topics/functions: Improving oneself; describing changes and exchanging personal information

Structures: Describing changes with the present tense, past tense, and present perfect

Summary

The sequence opens with Marty and John studying in the library. John asks Marty a question about a calculus problem. At that point, a young woman named Michelle approaches, greets John warmly, and invites him to study with her. John suggests that Michelle study with Marty because John is not working on the same chapter as Michelle. However, Michelle is clearly not interested. Marty is upset by this. He tells John about his frustration with women, explaining that they never seem interested in him. He then asks John for advice. John suggests Marty's problem may be due in part to his appearance. Marty is wearing old, torn clothes and has long, unkempt hair. The following scenes show Marty getting a haircut and new clothes, shaving, and exercising with John. Next, Marty and John are seen getting lunch in the school cafeteria. Michelle appears and greets John, once again asking him if he would like to study with her. John declines, but he repeats his suggestion that she and Marty study together. Michelle appears pleasantly surprised to see the new and improved Marty, and she happily agrees to study with him. Marty and Michelle walk off together.

 **Preview**

1 CULTURE

In the United States and Canada, it is widely accepted that people can substantially change their lives simply by making changes to their appearance or personality. The culture preview in the Video Activity Book introduces the topic of self-improvement and describes some self-improvement products and programs available.

■ Books closed. Ask the class, "Who has changed their hairstyle recently?" Have students respond by raising their hands to indicate they have.

■ Ask, "Who works out on exercise machines?" Again, have students respond by raising their hands.

■ On the board, write the following:
  Making changes

■ Put students in groups to list the things people usually want to change about themselves. Circulate to help with vocabulary questions. Have the groups share their lists with the class. Write these on the board to form a class list.

Possible answers
hair
health
skin
energy level
fitness
body shape
image
clothes
confidence
ability to make friends
being shy

■ Books open. Have students read the information in the culture preview silently. Then tell them to underline the term (*self-improvement*) that means "making changes to oneself."

■ Put students in pairs or small groups to work with the questions. Then ask several students to share their answers with the class.

2 **VOCABULARY** *Verb and noun pairs*

In these activities, students match verbs relating to self-improvement with the words or phrases they are usually used with.

A *Pair work* Books open. Explain the task, and read through the list of verbs. Explain that some of the verbs can be paired with more than one word or phrase, and vice versa.

■ Have students work in pairs to choose a verb (or verbs) to go with each word or phrase.

■ Have pairs of students compare answers with other pairs. Check the answers as a class, discussing all the possible variations.

Answers

1) change/improve my appearance
2) meet more people
3) make/meet more friends
4) gain/lose weight
5) do/get more exercise
6) buy/get/make (sew) some new clothes
7) change/improve my hairstyle
8) cut my hair
9) get in shape
10) gain/lose confidence

B Books open. Explain the task. Have students individually circle the words or phrases that describe the changes they would like to make about themselves.

■ Put students in pairs to compare the words and phrases they circled.

Optional activity

Books open. Have students make a chart listing self-improvement changes in a column on the left side of the paper, with five other columns on the right, headed by the following categories: Men, Women, Under 20 years old, Between 20 and 40, Over 40. Divide the class into groups and have the students fill in their charts by checking the changes they think apply to each group. When the groups have finished filling in their charts, ask students if they can make any generalizations about their findings, such as "More women than men want to change their hairstyle." Have selected groups share their generalizations with the class. (15 minutes)

3 **GUESS THE STORY**

In this activity, students prepare to watch the sequence by using visual information to predict what happens as the story progresses.

■ Books open. Explain the task. Have students look at the photos of Marty and John, and explain that these two young men are students working on calculus in the library. Have students read the four descriptive phrases in the box silently. Check students' comprehension of the word *popular*. Explain that each phrase describes only one of the two young men.

■ Tell students, "Now we will watch the sequence without the sound. Decide which phrases describe Marty and which ones describe John."

■ Play the first few seconds of the video without the sound, stopping to point out which young man is Marty and which is John. Then play the first minute of the video with the sound off as students watch and complete the task.

■ Have students compare their answers in pairs before you go over them as a class. Tell students to compare Marty's and John's respective clothes and hairstyles. If students are unsure about the answer to (4), tell them they will be able to check their answer when they watch the video.

Answers

1) Marty
2) John
3) John
4) John

■ Have students discuss in pairs why they think Marty is unhappy.

Optional activity

Pair work Books open or closed. With the sound off, replay the first thirty seconds of the sequence. Stop the video, and fast-forward to the scene at the end of the sequence when Marty and Michelle are talking to each other. Put the students in pairs to list the changes they notice in Marty. Ask students to discuss, first, what they think happened to Marty to make him change and, second, how he made these changes. Accept all answers at this point. (5 minutes)

Watch the video

4 GET THE PICTURE

In these activities, students watch and listen to the entire sequence to decide whether general statements about the video sequence are true or false about John, Marty, and Michelle. They also listen for the information needed to correct the false statements.

A Books open. Explain the task, and lead students through the six statements in the box. Discuss the meaning of *outgoing*, if necessary.

■ Direct students' attention to the pictures of Marty and John once again to check that students know which student is Marty and which is John.

■ Play the entire sequence with the sound on. Have students complete the task while they watch.

■ Check to see if anyone needs to watch the sequence again to check their answers, and replay as needed. Then put students in pairs to compare answers.

B *Pair work* Have students work in pairs to correct the false statements. Tell students they can request scenes to be replayed, if needed.

Answers
1) True
2) False (Michelle knows Marty.)
3) False (John is still on Chapter 11. Michelle doesn't study with John.)
4) True
5) False (Michelle doesn't recognize Marty.)
6) False (Marty and Michelle study together.)

Optional activity

■ *Pair work* Books closed. Have students watch the sequence again and then work with a partner to write two more statements about the sequence: one true and one false (e.g., "Marty needs to study for a history test." [False]; "John thinks Marty needs more energy." [True]).

■ Have pairs exchange papers, mark each other's statements as true or false, and return each other's papers to check them. (10–15 minutes)

5 WATCH FOR DETAILS

In this activity, students watch and listen for the specific information needed to answer questions about Marty's self-improvement plan.

■ Books open. Explain the task, and lead students through the six illustrations. Students can check the pictures they think are correct from memory first.

■ Tell students, "Now, watch and listen for the things Marty does to improve his appearance." With the sound on, play the part of the sequence in which Marty is seen actively trying to improve himself, while students complete the task.

■ Have students compare answers with a partner. Check answers around the class.

Answers
He lifts weights.
He gets a haircut.
He buys new clothes.
He shaves.

Optional activity

Books open. Have students watch the sequence again, this time from the point where Marty and John start exercising. Tell students to number the four relevant illustrations in the order in which they occur. Tell students to relabel the illustration of lifting weights to read "He exercises." (Write this on the board.) Also tell students to number that picture each time Marty is seen exercising. Put the students in pairs to compare answers. Check answers as a class. (10 minutes)

Answers
He exercises: 1, 3, 5
He shaves: 2
He buys new clothes: 4
He gets a haircut: 6

Follow-up

6 *WHAT HAPPENED?*

In these extension activities, students retell the
story of the sequence in their own words.

A *Pair work* Books closed. Ask students,
"Where are Marty and John in the first and last
scenes of the sequence?" Elicit that Marty and
John are in the college library at the beginning of
the sequence and in the college cafeteria at the
end. Tell students they will be retelling the
complete story of the sequence in their own
words.

■ Books open. Explain the task. Put students in
pairs to look at the pictures and to describe to
each other what they see in each one.

■ Read the starting line to the students. Explain
that the photos are there to guide the students,
but that they are free to add other details, if they
wish.

■ Have students tell each other the story, using
the pictures to guide them.

Possible answers
1) John and Michelle were in the library.
2) Michelle asked John for help with calculus (but
   she didn't want to study with Marty).
3) John gave Marty advice about girls and his
   appearance.
4) Marty went to the gym and exercised.
5) Marty bought some new clothes.
6) Michelle and Marty decided to study together
   for the calculus exam.

B Books open. Put pairs of students together
with other pairs to compare their stories. Have
selected pairs share their stories with the class.

Optional activity

Pair work Books closed. Tell students that they
are going to imagine they are either Michelle,
Marty, or John, and that they are telling a friend
the story of what happened. Put students in pairs
to take turns retelling the story from this new
perspective. Suggest that students add details
about how they were feeling at different points.
For example, Michelle might say she first felt
uncomfortable about studying with Marty and
made an excuse. Put the following starting lines
on the board.

Michelle: I was in the library and I saw . . .
Marty: I was in the library with John when
Michelle . . .
John: I was in the library with Marty
and . . .

Have selected students retell their stories.
(10 minutes)

7 GOOD ADVICE

In this activity, students have the opportunity to give suggestions to resolve specific personal problems.

■ Books open. Explain the task. Have students read the four situations. Check that students know that Tony is the only male name listed.

■ Model the sample language, using Marty as an example. Say, for example, "It's helpful to shave. It's a good idea to buy new clothes."

■ Put students in pairs to think of suggestions for Maria, Tina, Tony, and Karen. Put pairs together to compare their suggestions.

■ Go over the suggestions as a class. Ask groups to tell you how many suggestions they had for each person. Make a master list on the board.

Possible answers

1) She could join a singles club/use the Internet/ask her friends for help/try to be more outgoing.
2) She should get a tutor/ask her teacher for help. It's a good idea to study with a friend.
3) It might be helpful to join some clubs/think of things to talk about before going out with friends.
4) She should join a fitness club/go to the gym/exercise more.

Optional activity

Pair work Books closed. Tell students to think of three more problems that someone might have. Put them in pairs to write these problems on a piece of paper, using the sentences in the book as a guide. Have the pairs exchange papers with another pair. Once they have decided on appropriate advice, have them tell each other their advice. Have selected groups share their problems and advice with the class. (10 minutes)

 Language close-up

8 WHAT DID THEY SAY?

This cloze activity has students complete the conversation between Marty, John, and Michelle as they watch and listen to the video sequence.

■ Books open. Read the instructions. Have students read through the conversation individually or in pairs, filling in any blanks they can before watching the sequence.

■ Play the appropriate scene in the sequence with the sound on, while students both check the answers they filled in prior to listening and listen for the information needed to fill in the remaining blanks. Replay the scene as many times as needed.

■ Put students in groups of three to compare their answers. Go over the answers as a class, having the students repeat the lines with the correct intonation and pronunciation.

■ Working in the same groups, have students each choose one of the three roles and practice the conversation. Have selected groups act out the conversation for the class.

Answers

John: I'm just **terrible** at calculus. I don't **understand** anything in this **chapter**.

Marty: I **know** what you **mean**. It is a **tough** course.

John: Did you **figure** out the answer to this **problem**?

Marty: That's in Chapter 11. I **did** that **last** week. Let's see.

Michelle: Hi, John. I **see** you're **working** on calculus.

John: Oh, hi, Michelle. Yes, I **am**. Michelle, you **know** Marty, **don't** you?

Michelle: Yeah, hi, Marty. Say, John, I've got a **couple** of **questions** about Chapter 12. Do you want to **study** together?

John: Well, uh, actually, I'm **still** on Chapter 11, but Marty **here** is working on Chapter 12.

Michelle: Oh, that's OK. Actually, I've **got to** go to class **right** now. See you **later**.

John: OK, Michelle. **See you**.

Optional activities

A *Group work* Books closed. Have students act out the parts of Marty, John, and Michelle without looking at their books. Explain that it is not important to use the exact words from the sequence. Have the groups practice their conversations. Invite students to perform their role plays for the class. (10 minutes)

B *Pair work* Books closed. Play the scene a couple of times in which John and Marty discuss Marty's problem. Put students in pairs to write down John's and Marty's words as well as they can remember them. Again, tell students it is not important to use the exact words John and Marty used. Circulate to help students with vocabulary and structure. Have the pairs practice their dialogues and perform them for the class. (10 minutes)

---

9 *DESCRIBING CHANGES*

A In these activities, students complete sentences about changes people have made to their lives and then make similar sentences about themselves.

■ Books open. Explain the task. Have students read the list of words.

■ Put students in pairs to decide which words in the list are verbs and which ones are adjectives. Remind students that adjectives change their form when used as comparatives. Also remind students that the form of the verb will depend on whether the sentence is in the simple present, simple past, or present perfect.

■ Have students complete the sentences individually and then get into pairs to compare answers. Go over the answers as a class.

Answers
1) wear
2) drive
3) longer
4) busier
5) painted
6) started
7) bought
8) changed

B Books open. Explain the task, and give a sample sentence or two about yourself to demonstrate. Then have students work alone to write four sentences about themselves as you circulate to help.

■ Put students into pairs, and have them take turns reading their sentences.

■ When students seem satisfied, bring the class back together. Call on individual students to share their sentences with the class.

Optional activity

Pair work Books closed. Write the following words and phrases on the board.

exercise	cut	shave	wear
lift weights	short	buy	

With the sound off, play the scene in the sequence that shows the "whole new Marty" talking to Michelle in the cafeteria. Tell students to imagine that they are Marty and to make sentences about how they (Marty) have changed themselves, using the words and phrases on the board.

Possible answers
I exercise now.
I lift weights.
I've cut my hair.
My hair is shorter.
Now I shave every day.
I've bought some new clothes.
I wear neater clothes.

What is American food?

Preview

1 CULTURE

American food is not limited to one kind of food, but is a variety of foods. Each region of the United States has its own special dishes depending on the ethnic mix of its people. When Americans go out to eat they are most likely to order Italian, Chinese, or Mexican foods. These types of foods are popular with nearly everyone. The culture preview in the Video Activity Book introduces the topic of American food by presenting some background information and essential vocabulary.

■ Books closed. On the board write: What is American food? Have students work in pairs to write their answers. (Note: Do not be concerned if answers vary.)

■ Have pairs form small groups to compare responses. Then ask several groups to share their answers with the class.

■ Books open. Have students read the culture preview silently to compare their answers with the information presented.

■ Ask questions such as these around the class: "What foods are popular in America? Why are there many different kinds of foods in the United States?" Have selected students answer.

■ Ask several students to respond to the questions, or have students work in pairs to take turns asking and answering the questions before talking about them as a class.

Watch the video

2 GET THE PICTURE

In this activity, students watch and listen to identify the kinds of restaurants that serve various foods that are popular in the United States.

■ Books open. Explain the task, and have students look at each of the six pictures.

■ Have students work alone to predict the answers and then compare their answers with a partner.

■ Play the entire sequence with the sound on. Have students work alone to check and correct their predictions while they watch.

■ Have students compare their answers with a partner or around the class.

■ Play the documentary again, and have students check their answers. Then go over them with the class.

Answers
1) G, bratwurst   4) C, Kung-pao chicken
2) CA, Caesar salad   5) CA, pasta
3) A, a hamburger   6) C, pork Szechwan

Optional activities

A *Pair work* Books open. Have pairs take turns asking and answering questions about which of these foods they have eaten. Encourage students to ask about other foods as well. (5 minutes)

Possible dialogue
A: Have you ever eaten bratwurst?
B: Yes, I have. Have you ever eaten . . . ?

B *Pair work* Books closed. Play the documentary without the sound, and have students, working in pairs, choose one of the restaurants. Then replay the sequence a few more times, and have the pairs list all of the things that they can see people doing or eating in the restaurant that they choose. (10 minutes)

Possible answers (for the German restaurant)
People are listening to music and watching the entertainers (A man and two women are singing and dancing.).
People are eating many different German foods, including Bavarian goulash, German cabbage and potato salad, and bratwurst.
Waitresses are carrying large trays and baskets of food.

3 WATCH FOR DETAILS

In this activity, students focus on details by watching and listening in order to match photos of people from the documentary with the names of foods that they ate.

■ Books open. Explain the task, and have students look through the photos.

■ Play the entire sequence, as students work to complete the task.

■ Have students compare answers with a partner, and then go over the answers with the class.

Answers
1) chicken salad
2) Caesar salad
3) pasta
4) Kung-pao chicken
5) pork Szechwan
6) Bavarian goulash

4 IT'S ALL AMERICAN FOOD

In this activity, students focus on details by watching and listening in order to answer four questions about American food.

■ Books open. Explain the task, and read through the questions with the class.

■ Play the sequence while students watch and listen for the answers as they view.

■ Have students compare their answers with a partner, and then replay the documentary if necessary.

■ Check students' answers around class.

Answers
1) fresh fruits and vegetables.
2) a self-service buffet.
3) listen to music and eat.
4) a hamburger and french fries.

 *Follow-up*

5 HOW ABOUT YOU?

In this activity, students extend and personalize the information in this sequence by asking and answering questions about foods and restaurants.

■ Books open. Explain the task, and read through the questions with the class.

■ *Group work* Put students into small groups to take turns asking and answering the questions.

■ Bring the class back together, and have various group members share their answers with the class.

Optional activity

■ *Group work* Books open or closed. Have students work in small groups to write three questions about foods and restaurants.

■ Have two groups work together, taking turns asking and answering each other's questions. Then have each group share their most interesting question and answer with the class. (10 minutes)

Possible questions
Would you rather eat in a restaurant or at home?
What's your favorite fast-food restaurant?
Do you like listening to music while you eat?

1 First day at class

Rick starts class at a university and gets a surprise.

Marie: I'm sorry, Miss Tanaka. What's your first name again?

Sachiko: Sachiko. S-A-C-H-I-K-O.

Marie: Thanks. See you in a minute.

Rick: Hi. My name's Ricardo, but everybody calls me Rick.

Marie: Well, nice to meet you, Rick. I'm Marie Ouellette.

Rick: It's nice to meet you, Marie. . . . Um, where are you from, Marie?

Marie: I'm from Canada.

Rick: Oh, so you're Canadian?

Marie: That's right.

Rick: From what city?

Marie: Montreal. How about you?

Rick: I'm originally from Mexico City, but my family and I live up here now.

Marie: Oh, are you a student here?

Rick: Yes, I am.

Marie: What are you studying?

Rick: Business Management.

Marie: Oh, really! That's nice.

Rick: So, how about you? Are you a student, too?

Marie: Well, no, . . .

Rick: So, what do you do?

Marie: I teach.

Rick: Oh? What do you teach?

Marie: Business Management.

• • •

Sachiko: Excuse me, Miss Ouellette. This is our classroom, isn't it?

Marie: Yes, Sachiko, it is. Nice to meet you, Rick. Bye-bye!

Rick: Yeah, you too! Good-bye.

2 I need a change!

Lynn dreams about a new career.

Paula: Hi, Lynn! How are you doing?

Lynn: Oh, hi, Paula. Pretty good, thanks. How are you?

Paula: Not bad. Say, you know Bob Wallace, don't you?

Lynn: Oh, no, I don't think so. Hi, I'm Lynn Parker.

Bob: Pleased to meet you.

Paula: So, how's everything?

Lynn: Do you really want to know?

Paula: Of course I do.

Lynn: Well, it's my job.

Paula: But you have a great job.

Bob: Where do you work, Lynn?

Lynn: At AdTech.

Bob: What kind of business is that?

Lynn: It's a computer software company.

Bob: So, what do you do?

Lynn: I'm a manager in customer service.

Bob: Well, that sounds interesting.

Lynn: Well, . . . it is, but I'm at the office ten hours a day, six days a week. I'm always on the phone or at the computer. I need a change.

Paula: Well, what do you want to do, Lynn?

Lynn: Actually, I want to work in a hotel.

Paula: A hotel?

Lynn: In fact, I'm studying hotel management.

Paula: Really?

Lynn: Yes, I take evening classes.

Paula: Well, that's great!

Lynn: And when I finish, I want to find a job in a warm climate.

Bob: You do? How about a job in Hawaii?

Lynn: Hawaii?

Bob: Sure. I have a friend who manages a hotel in Honolulu.

Lynn: Really?

Bob: Yeah. Maybe he has a job for you.

Paula: Hawaii . . . well, that sounds great. . . . Oh, excuse me, I've got to get back to work.

Lynn: Oh. OK, Paula. Bye.

Bob: Take it easy, Paula.

Paula: See you later.

Lynn: Hawaii . . .

Jobs

People talk about what they do as we watch them at work.

Reporter: Hi. I'm Mike Sullivan for KNOW News Seven. This is the Minneapolis Skyway. People use these skyways to go to and from their jobs. Now, let's go to where they work and see what kinds of jobs they have.

• • •

Architect: Hi. My name's Rob Reis, and I'm an architect.

• • •

Lawyer: Hi. I'm Laurie Peterson, and I'm a lawyer.

• • •

Pianist: Hello. My name is Vladimir Lavitsky, and I'm the pianist of the Minnesota Orchestra.

• • •

Computer engineer: Hi. I'm Pete Ketchum, and I'm a computer engineer.

• • •

Cashier: Hi. My name is Cookie. I'm a part-time cashier at Byerly's.

• • •

Bank teller: Hi. I'm Shannon Bruin, and I'm a bank teller.

• • •

Doctor: Hello. My name is Dr. Mari Eto. I work in an emergency room.

• • •

Chef: Hi. My name is James Williams, and I'm a chef. It's a great job, and I love it.

• • •

Photographer: Hi. My name's Rick Armstrong, and I'm a commercial photographer. Welcome to my studio. . . . I photograph people and things. Mainly, I photograph people for magazines, and I photograph famous people for interviews. I enjoy meeting people. . . . I also take pictures of things for advertisements, like shampoo and soap. . . . It's an exciting job; there's something different every day. But it's really hard work. . . . Sometimes to get a good picture, I have to take fifty or sixty different shots of exactly the same thing. It's certainly a challenge.

• • •

Travel-agency owner: Hello. I'm Sylvia Davis. I own Worldwide Travel. We plan tours to more than fifty different countries, and sometimes I spend all day talking on the phone and writing faxes. . . . We're a small business with only three travel agents, so it's very busy here. A business is a big responsibility, but I get to travel, too. Several times a year my travel agents and I go to different countries to look at new hotels. I love to travel! It's interesting and always different. How about you, do you like your job?

• • •

Reporter: Those are a few of the interesting jobs people have here in Minneapolis. This is Mike Sullivan for KNOW News Seven.

3 At a garage sale

Fred and Susan have different opinions about things at a garage sale.

Fred: Hey, Susan, how do you like this?

Susan: Oh, please, Fred.

Fred: Oh, come on. It's only a dollar!

Susan: Do you really want it, Fred?

Fred: No, I guess you're right.

· · ·

Vendor: Can I help you?

Fred: No, thanks anyway. We're just looking.

Susan: Oh, Fred, come over here. Just look at this lovely, old necklace!

Fred: Yeah, it's OK.

Susan: It's not just OK, Fred. It's very nice! . . . And look at this bracelet. Excuse me, how much are these?

Vendor: Oh, let's see. How about fifteen dollars for the two of them?

Fred: Oh, that's not bad.

Susan: And how much is that old watch?

Vendor: This one? Oh, this one is, uh, twenty-five dollars.

Fred: Susan, are you kidding? Twenty-five dollars for that old watch?

Vendor: This watch is old, but it still runs. Listen!

Susan: How old is it?

Vendor: Oh, I don't really know. But it's very old.

Susan: Oh, it is lovely. . . . I'll take it.

Fred: OK!

Vendor: Do you want those, too?

Susan: Yes, I'll take these, too.

Vendor's husband: Marge, is that my mother's watch?

Vendor: What? . . . I don't know!

Vendor's husband: It is my mother's watch! Excuse me, but this watch is not for sale. I'm sorry. . . . Marge, could you come over here, please? (*to Fred and Susan*) I'm sorry.

· · ·

Fred: Hey, Susan, look at this!

Susan: Oh, no, Fred. Not the motorcycle!

4 What kind of movies do you like?

Bill, Alfredo, and Pat try to agree on what they should do one evening.

Bill: So, . . . what do we do now?

Alfredo: What time is it?

Bill: Seven o'clock.

Pat: Look, we all like movies. Why don't we rent a video and watch it at my house?

Bill: That's not a bad idea, Pat.

Alfredo: It's OK with me.

Pat: Well, then, come on! . . . Now here are some great science-fiction movies! What do you think, Bill?

Bill: Uh, I can't stand sci-fi. How about a good suspense thriller?

Pat: Uh . . . Alfredo, what about you? What do you think of science fiction?

Alfredo: Oh, it's OK.

Bill: Well, what kind of movies *do* you like?

Alfredo: I really like classic films a lot.

Pat: Then come over here. There are some great old horror films here with some of my favorite actors.

Alfredo: Really? I love horror films!

Bill: A fifty-year-old movie! Are you kidding?

Pat: Well, then, how about a western? Do you like westerns?

Bill: A western?

Alfredo: Wait a minute. I think I have an answer to our problem.

Pat: What problem?

Alfredo: Well, we can't agree on a movie, right?

Bill: Well, . . .

Alfredo: How about some music? There's a terrific group at the Cafe Solo tonight.

Bill: Yeah. That sounds good.

Pat: Sure. Why not?

Alfredo: Well, then, let's go!

• • •

Bill: So, what's the name of this rock group?

Alfredo: It's not a rock group. It's a country and western group.

Bill: Country and western?

Alfredo: Yeah.

Bill: Well, gee, I . . . I really don't like country and western very much . . .

Pat: Isn't there a jazz concert at the City Center tonight?

Bill: Jazz? Do you really like jazz?

What's your favorite kind of music?

People talk about their preferences in music as they listen to and watch live performances.

Reporter: Hi. I'm Austene Van Williams, and I'm in front of a country and western nightclub. Let's talk to some people and see what they think of the music.

• • •

Reporter: How do you like this music?

Woman 1: We love it. We love it.

Reporter: What kind of music do they play here?

Woman 1: Country. Country music.

Reporter: And how often do you get to go to nightclubs?

Woman 1: Well, we just come here mostly about . . . uh, two times a week.

Reporter: What's your favorite kind of music?

Man 1: Country western.

Reporter: Country western?

Man 1: Yeah.

• • •

Reporter: What's *your* favorite kind of music?

Man 2: Country western. The old time, hard-core country western. Western swing. And my least favorite is rap.

Reporter: Rap?

Man 2: I . . . I don't understand it. It makes me feel old.

• • •

Reporter: What's your favorite kind of music?

Woman 2: I really enjoy country music. I like a variety of music, though, so . . .

Reporter: How often do you listen to live music?

Woman 2: Um . . . couple of times a month, maybe.

• • •

Reporter: What's your favorite kind of music?

Man 3: Uh . . . if I say country – no, it's not country. It's probably jazz.

Reporter: Jazz?

Man 3: Right.

Woman 3: Uh . . . jazz.

• • •

Reporter: What kind of music do they play here?

Woman 4: They play jazz.

Man 4: Uh . . . almost always jazz. Some blues.

Reporter: What's your favorite kind of music?

Man 5: My favorite's older rock, uh, new wave. I like jazz a lot, too.

Woman 5: I like classical music and jazz.

Woman 6: I like jazz music, and I also like rock and roll.

Man 5: I like jazz music.

Reporter: How often do you go to nightclubs?

Man 5: Um, I come here about once a month.

Reporter: What's your least favorite kind of music?

Man 5: I don't like country western music.

Woman 5: I don't like country music, and I don't like rock and roll.

Man 4: I really dislike Top 40.

Reporter: Do you play a musical instrument yourself?

Man 4: No, I don't.

Woman 6: Yes, I do. I play the guitar.

Man 5: I play saxophone.

Woman 5: Yes, I play piano.

• • •

Reporter: I think the people here may have a few different opinions about music. . . . How do you like this music?

Man 6: I enjoy it a lot.

Reporter: What kind of music do they play here?

Man 6: A lot of rock. A lot of R & B. It's usually good music.

Reporter: How often do you go to nightclubs?

Man 6: Pretty often. Whenever I get a day off work.

Reporter: How often do you go to nightclubs?

Man 7: Mm . . . once a week, maybe.

Reporter: What's your favorite kind of music?

Man 7: Rock.

Reporter: Rock?

Man 7: Yes.

Reporter: What do you think of country and western music?

Man 7: Uh . . . it's not my favorite. It's OK, but I don't, I don't buy it, and I don't listen to it too often, though.

Reporter: Do you play a musical instrument yourself?

Man 7: Um-hmm.

Reporter: What instrument is that?

Man 7: The guitar.

Reporter: The guitar? Well, thank you very much.

Man 7: You're welcome.

Reporter: What kind of music do they play here?

Woman 7: Great music. Dancing music.

•   •   •

Reporter: And that's what people think of the music here. I think I'll go back for some more rock and roll. Bye now.

5 A family picnic

Rick invites Betsy to a family picnic.

Betsy: So, how many people are there in your family, Rick?

Rick: A lot, if you count all my cousins.

Betsy: Do they all live here in the States now?

Rick: Oh, no. I have relatives in Mexico. My grandmother and grandfather are there, and my older sister, too.

Betsy: How many sisters do you have?

Rick: Two, plus an older brother. There's my brother Freddy over there with his wife Linda.

Betsy: Oh, really. What do they do?

Rick: Freddy has an import-export business, and Linda manages a boutique.

Betsy: Is that their daughter?

Rick: Yeah. Her name's Angela.

Betsy: She's cute. How old is she?

Rick: She's three.

• • •

Rick: Betsy, I'd like you to meet my mother and father.

Betsy: Pleased to meet you.

Mrs. Hernandez: Hi, Betsy.

Mr. Hernandez: Nice to meet you, Betsy.

Betsy: Hello, Mr. Hernandez.

Rick: And this is my younger sister Cristina.

Cristina: Hi, Betsy.

Betsy: Hi, Cristina.

Rick: Aunt Marta, this is my friend Betsy Scott, from the night school class.

Betsy: Hi.

Aunt Marta: Well, nice to meet you, Betsy. Can you two please come with me? It's time for the family picture.

Rick: Sure.

Aunt Marta: Come on, please, everyone!

• • •

Betsy: Can I take the picture for you? Then you can be in it, too.

Aunt Marta: Oh, thank you, Betsy! Now here's the camera. I hope it works OK. It's . . . it's an old one.

Betsy: Oh, no problem. . . . Listen, everybody. I want you to say "cheese" on three. One . . . two . . . three!

Family: Cheese!

6 I like to stay in shape.

Mark tries to impress Anne by telling her about his fitness routine.

Mark: Hi there. Nice day, isn't it?

Anne: Oh, yes, very nice.

Mark: Do you often come out here this early?

Anne: Usually. I like to stay in shape.

Mark: I do, too. I usually get up around five o'clock.

Anne: Oh, really?

Mark: Yeah. I usually start with some stretches. There's a great aerobics program on TV at six.

Anne: No kidding. I guess you really do like to stay in shape.

Mark: Hey, three days a week I go straight to my health club after work.

Anne: Wow. What do you do the other two evenings?

Mark: Tuesdays and Thursdays, I'm on the old tennis courts by five-thirty.

Anne: Well, after all that exercise during the week, what do you do over the weekend?

Mark: Saturdays and Sundays are my days for team sports.

• • •

Nancy: Hi, Anne. Are we late?

Anne: Oh, no, Nancy. You're . . . right on time. Hi, Terry.

Terry: Are you ready for a couple more miles?

Anne: Sure. Say, . . . would you like to join us?

Mark: Oh, no. . . . Uh, thanks, anyway. I don't have time today. Sorry.

Anne: OK. Well, bye-bye. Have a nice day!

• • •

Mark: *(to new person)* Hi there. Nice day, isn't it?

7 How was your trip to San Francisco?

Phyllis tells Yoko about her trip to San Francisco.

Yoko: Hi, Phyllis.

Phyllis: Hi, Yoko. How have you been?

Yoko: Oh, fine. How about you?

Phyllis: Great! Just great!

Yoko: So how was your trip to San Francisco?

Phyllis: Fantastic! We really enjoyed it.

Yoko: Well, that doesn't surprise me. I love to visit San Francisco. Uh, so, your husband went with you?

Phyllis: Yes. I worked on Friday, and Bill had business to do in the city, too.

Yoko: Oh, that's nice. So what did you do over the weekend?

Phyllis: We went sight-seeing together all day Saturday and Sunday morning.

Yoko: Oh, really? Tell me about it.

Phyllis: Well, we did a lot of interesting things. Naturally, we started Saturday morning with a ride on a cable car.

Yoko: Naturally. . . . And then?

Phyllis: Then we went straight to Ghirardelli Square to do some shopping.

Yoko: Isn't it wonderful? I went there the last time I was in San Francisco.

Phyllis: Oh, it sure is. We were there for a couple of hours.

Yoko: Did you buy anything?

Phyllis: Just some postcards and chocolate. We didn't want to have too much to carry.

Yoko: What did you do after that?

Phyllis: We had lunch at a crab stand at Fisherman's Wharf.

Yoko: Did you visit Alcatraz Island?

Phyllis: No, we didn't have time.

Yoko: Oh, . . . what did you do then?

Phyllis: We took a cab to Golden Gate Park.

Yoko: Great! Did you see the Japanese Tea Garden?

Phyllis: Oh, yes, it was really beautiful. . . . But to tell the truth, the thing we liked the best was Chinatown.

Yoko: Oh, really?

Phyllis: Yes. We went there on Sunday morning.

Yoko: What did you like about Chinatown?

Phyllis: Well, . . . all the people, . . . and the buildings, the shops, and restaurants . . . even the way the streets look. It was just a fascinating place. We walked for hours.

Yoko: I know what you mean. It sounds like you really had fun.

Phyllis: Oh, we had a great time! So how about you? What did you do over the weekend?

Yoko: Oh, nothing much. Well, here we are again.

Phyllis: Oh, back to the real world!

8 Are you sure it's all right?

Bill invites two friends to a party and finds out that he has made a mistake.

Sandy: Are you sure it's all right for us to go to the party?

Bill: Of course I am. Katy's a good friend of mine.

Sandy: Yes, but she didn't really invite Pat and me, and it is a little late.

Bill: It's OK, Sandy. It's a very informal party, . . . and anyway she knows both of you already.

Pat: OK. Well, we're at the corner of 31st Street. Now what?

Bill: Well, I don't remember her address, but I know she lives near here.

Pat: Fine. But do I go left, right, or straight ahead?

Bill: Straight ahead. . . . I remember there's a movie theater just before you turn.

Pat: Hey, is that it?

Bill: No, I don't think so. . . . There was a coffee shop next door and a drugstore across the street.

Sandy: Oh, I don't see a drugstore. Well, there's a Vietnamese restaurant . . . with a bookstore next to it.

Pat: Yeah, and no coffee shop either. Hey, look! There's another movie theater up ahead on the left.

Bill: Great! There's a drugstore.

•   •   •

Bill: We're almost there. . . . Turn left at the corner. . . . There's a parking lot just to the left. . . . There it is!

Pat: Great!

•   •   •

Pat: So where does Katy live?

Bill: In one of those apartment buildings across the street.

Pat: Which one?

Bill: It's the one on the corner.

•   •   •

Sandy: And you're sure it's all right for us to arrive this late?

Bill: Come on, Sandy!

Sandy: I don't hear any music!

Katy: Bill?

Bill: Hi, Katy.

Katy: Hi.

Bill: Are we too late for the party?

Katy: Oh, no. . . . Uh, actually, you're a little early.

Bill: Really?

Katy: Yes. The party is next Friday.

Bill: Next Friday?

Katy: Yes. Hi, Sandy. Pat. Come on in.

Sandy: I'm sorry, Katy.

Pat: Are you sure it's all right?

Katy: No problem. . . . It looks like we have a party here tonight after all.

In a suburban home

A woman talks about her home as she walks through each room.

Reporter: Homes in North America come in all shapes and sizes. Hi. I'm Donna Fox. Today we're going to look at a typical home in the midwestern United States. Homes are often very large in the Midwest. As you can see, there's a lot of room to build houses here. The Bartlett family lives in this two-story suburban home. Let's go inside and meet Marcy Bartlett.

• • •

Reporter: Hi, Marcy. Thanks for inviting us to see your house.

Marcy: You're welcome, Donna. Thank you for coming.

Reporter: Are you ready to begin our tour?

Marcy: Sure. This, of course, is our kitchen, where we have most of our family meals.

Reporter: How many people are in your family?

Marcy: There's four: my husband Bob, my two children, and myself.

Reporter: What other rooms are on the ground floor?

Marcy: Well, we have the formal dining room right through here.

Reporter: And when do you use this room?

Marcy: We use it mostly for entertaining and special family dinners.

Reporter: It's lovely.

Marcy: Thank you.

• • •

Marcy: And we have our living room here on the main floor also.

Reporter: Oh, I like it! What's on the second floor?

Marcy: We have four bedrooms upstairs. Would you like to go and see?

Reporter: Yes.

• • •

Marcy: And this is my son Matthew's room. He's five.

Reporter: Oh, it's really nice!

• • •

Marcy: And over here we have the guest room.

• • •

Marcy: And down here we have the children's bathroom.

Reporter: OK.

• • •

Marcy: And over here is my son Daniel's room. . . . He's eight.

Reporter: Oh. . . . Oh, your son has lots of trophies. Where did he get them?

Marcy: He takes karate.

Reporter: Oh.

• • •

Marcy: And through here . . . is our bedroom.

Reporter: Well, you have lots of room up here. Where does the family spend the most time?

Marcy: Oh, that's easy, Donna. Down in the family room. Come on and I'll show you.

Reporter: OK.

• • •

Reporter: What a great family room!

Marcy: Thank you. The boys love to play down here, and we spend a lot of time watching TV, playing games . . .

Reporter: Well, thank you so much for the tour, Marcy.

Marcy: You're welcome, Donna. Thank you for coming.

9 Help is coming.

Sarah and Dave are relaxing at home when they are surprised by visitors.

Sarah: Would you like another cup of coffee?

Dave: No, thanks. I don't think so.

Sarah: Is there anything interesting in the paper?

Dave: Well, there's something about a prison escape.

Sarah: Oh, really?

Dave: Yeah. A couple of guys escaped from the state prison in a gray van.

Sarah: Hmm. . . . Do we know anyone with a minivan?

Dave: A minivan? What color is it?

Sarah: I don't know. Light blue, maybe, or gray. I can't see very well.

Dave: Where is this van?

Sarah: It's parked right in front of the house. And there are two guys in it.

Dave: Oh, really?

Sarah: Now they're getting out of the van.

Dave: What do they look like?

Sarah: Well, . . . one man's tall, and I think he has blond hair. He's wearing a baseball cap.

Dave: How about the other one?

Sarah: He's . . . short. . . . He's got dark hair. Now they're coming up the driveway.

Dave: Sarah, you keep watching. I'm going to call the police.

Sarah: I think that's a good idea.

• • •

Dave: What are they doing now?

Sarah: They've stopped in the driveway and they're just looking around.

Dave: About how old are they? Can, can you tell?

Sarah: Well, the tall one looks like he's about twenty, and I guess the short one's in his late forties. Oh, Dave, now they're coming up to the door. Hurry!

Dave: It's all right, Sarah. Help is coming.

Sarah: Wait a minute! I can really see them now. . . . Oh, Dave! . . . The short one is your cousin George.

Dave: My cousin George!

• • •

George: Dave! So this is the right address. It's been so long since I've seen you, I wasn't sure.

Dave: George! What on earth are you doing here?

Sarah: Please, come in!

George: We were passing through town and decided to stop and say hello. You haven't seen Don here since he was a baby.

Don: Hi.

Sarah: Well, it's great to see you both again. . . . Dave, I think you should make that phone call, don't you?

Dave: Uh, sure. Please excuse me a minute.

Sarah: Dave'll be right back. Come in and sit down.

10 Sorry I'm late.

On his way to meet Marie, Tom has a problem.

Waitress: Good evening.

Marie: Hi. There will be two of us. . . . Thank you. . . .

Tom: Marie! I'm really sorry. How long have you been waiting?

Marie: It's OK, Tom. I've only been here for a little while. Is everything all right?

Tom: Yes, it is now, but you won't believe what just happened to me.

Marie: Well, what happened?

Tom: Well, first of all, I was a little late leaving my apartment, and so I was in a hurry. Then, just after I started the car, I remembered I didn't have any money with me, so I went back to get my wallet.

Marie: Did you find it?

Tom: Oh, yes. I found it. That wasn't the problem. The problem was when I got back to my car, I couldn't get in.

Marie: Do you mean you locked your keys in the car?

Tom: That's right. So, guess what I did after that!

Marie: I can't guess.

Tom: First I tried to call you, but there was no answer. . . . Then I called one of those twenty-four-hour lock services, . . . and they sent a man over to help me.

Marie: And he opened your car door for you?

Tom: That's right.

Marie: How long did it take?

Tom: About two minutes. So, I paid him and came straight here . . .

Marie: How much did this cost you?

Tom: Oh, it wasn't very expensive. It cost only – oh, no!

Marie: What is it?

Tom: My wallet! It's still in the car!

Marie: Oh!

Waitress: Good evening. Are you ready to order now?

Marie: Don't worry, Tom. You've had a hard day, and it's my turn to pay, anyway.

Tom: Thanks.

Marie: Let's see . . .

Tom: Well, should we start with an hors d'oeuvre?

Marie: Hm-hmm.

Tom: OK.

Across the Golden Gate Bridge

Mr. and Mrs. Chang get directions and advice as they rent a car at the airport.

Ken: Good morning. May I help you?

Mr. Chang: Yes, we're here to pick up a car.

Ken: Do you have a reservation?

Mr. Chang: Yes. The name is Chang.

Ken: OK, Chang, Chang. Here it is, Mr. Chang. Paid in advance. Sign here and here. And that's for one week then?

Mr. Chang: That's right. One week.

Ken: Are you staying in San Francisco?

Mrs. Chang: No, we're going to visit friends in the Napa Valley.

Ken: Oh, Napa Valley. That's one of my favorite places. The wineries and vineyards there are some of the most famous in California.

Mr. Chang: What's the best way to get there from here?

Mrs. Chang: Yes, and are there any interesting places to visit along the way?

Ken: The most interesting way is across the Golden Gate Bridge. It's not too crowded this time of day, and you can stop in Sausalito for lunch.

Mrs. Chang: Sausalito?

Ken: Yes. It's a fascinating little town just across the bridge. You should definitely see it.

Mrs. Chang: Can you recommend a good restaurant?

Ken: I really like Houlihan's. It's right on the waterfront, and there's a wonderful view of San Francisco across the bay.

Mr. Chang: So, Sausalito is on the way to the Napa Valley?

Ken: Yes, it is. And so is Muir Woods. You should stop there for a while, too, if you have time.

Mrs. Chang: Muir Woods?

Ken: Yes. It's a beautiful redwood forest. You shouldn't miss it.

Mrs. Chang: Mmm. Sounds interesting.

Mr. Chang: Well, thank you for the information. We'd better go find our car now.

Ken: That will be easy. Take the shuttle bus, just outside the door to the right. Here is your contract and directions to help you find the Golden Gate Bridge. Do you need anything else?

Mrs. Chang: No, we have everything that we need. Thank you so much.

Ken: OK. Good-bye. See you next week. . . . Oh, and be sure to visit one of the wineries up in Napa Valley.

Mr. Chang: Thanks. We will.

• • •

Mr. Chang: I just remembered. I don't have a map of the Napa Valley. Maybe I can get one here.

Mrs. Chang: Don't worry, dear. We can get one in Sausalito after lunch.

12 Feeling bad

Steve receives various home remedies for his cold from his co-workers.

Sandy: How are those papers coming for this afternoon, Steve?

Steve: Nearly finished.

Sandy: Do you still have that cold?

Steve: Yeah, it's still pretty bad, Sandy.

Sandy: Listen, I've got just the thing for you. Just a second. . . . Here.

Steve: What's that?

Sandy: It's something I picked up at the health-food store. You just mix it with hot water and drink it.

Steve: But what is it?

Sandy: I'm not really sure. I think it has ginseng in it or something like that. Try it.

Steve: Are you sure it works?

Sandy: Of course it does.

Steve: Well, thanks, Sandy. That's really nice. Maybe later.

Sandy: OK. . . . Oh, but don't drive after you take it.

Steve: Why not?

Sandy: It makes you sleepy.

Steve: Sleepy?

Sandy: Yeah, it's pretty strong medicine.

• • •

Jim: Hey, Steve. Still feeling bad?

Steve: Yes, it's this terrible cold.

Jim: No problem. I have something for you.

Steve: You do? Great.

Jim: Yeah, it's here in my briefcase. My mom makes it for me when I have a cold.

Steve: Really?

Jim: Here it is. Try it.

Steve: Umm, thanks, Jim. . . . Uh, what is it?

Jim: It's garlic juice. Actually, it's garlic, onions, and carrots.

Steve: Great.

Jim: Drink a cup of this every two hours. It's really great for a cold.

Steve: I'm sure. Gee, thanks, Jim.

Jim: Not at all. . . . Hope you feel better.

Steve: Thanks.

• • •

Rebecca: Well, Steve. How are you feeling now?

Steve: Oh, about the same, Rebecca.

Rebecca: Oh. . . . Listen, don't take any of this stuff. I have the best cure of all.

Steve: You do?

Rebecca: That's right. I'm taking you out to lunch to a place where they make the best chicken soup in the world.

Steve: What a good idea.

Rebecca: It is. So, come on, let's go.

Steve: You know, that's the best advice I've had all day, Rebecca. Just give me a minute to clean my desk. I'll meet you downstairs, OK?

Rebecca: OK. See you in a minute.

At the Mall of America

People talk about the largest mall in North America as they look and shop.

Reporter: Hi there. This is Neil Murray speaking to you from the Mall of America in Bloomington, Minnesota. And what is the Mall of America, you ask? Would you believe the biggest shopping and entertainment mall in the entire United States? Here at the Mall of America, you'll find four major department stores, all under the same roof. . . . Plus, hundreds of other places to shop. There are fourteen cinemas. . . . More than forty places to eat. . . . There's dancing. There's music. . . . And in the middle of everything, there's Camp Snoopy, an exciting amusement park.

• • •

Reporter: Now, let's ask some people what they're doing here. . . . Is this your first time at the Mall?

Woman 1: Yes, it is.

Reporter: Why are you here?

Woman 1: For Camp Snoopy, mainly. It's been really fun. We did a little bit of shopping and . . .

Reporter: What do you think people should do first when they come to the Mall of America?

Woman 1: Wear tennis shoes! . . . Wear tennis shoes. I didn't wear them.

• • •

Reporter: Have you been to the Mall of America before?

Woman 2: Uh, yeah, about three times.

Reporter: Why are you here now?

Woman 2: Because my mom came in from Ohio, and she wanted to go to the Mall of America.

Reporter: Have you purchased anything yet?

Woman 2: Yes. I bought a pair of shoes.

• • •

Reporter: What would you recommend for visitors from another country?

Woman 3: Well, this is a great place to come. I mean, there's everything. It's got everything in it, so if there's anything specific you're looking for, you can find it here.

• • •

Reporter: Hi.

Young girls: Hi.

Reporter: What's your name?

Ashley: Ashley.

Reporter: And you?

Corina: Corina.

Reporter: Where are you from?

Ashley: Oklahoma.

Corina: Oklahoma.

Reporter: What did you do when you got here?

Corina: We rode rides and looked at the stores.

Reporter: Have you eaten any food yet?

Ashley: No, we were too busy on the rides.

• • •

Reporter: May I ask you your name?

Hernando: Hi. Hernando.

Monica: Monica.

Rodrigo: Rodrigo.

Reporter: Where are you from?

Rodrigo: I'm from Ecuador. That's in South America.

Monica: Me, too. Ecuador.

Hernando: I am from Colombia, in South America, too.

Reporter: Why are you here at the Mall of America?

(continued)

Hernando: Ah, for shopping. Just now for shopping.

Reporter: Have you bought anything yet?

Rodrigo: Yeah. Just a couple of tapes.

Reporter: Well, where are they?

Rodrigo: They are over here. . . . Just the tapes. We're beginning.

Monica: Because we just arrived a few minutes ago.

Reporter: Are you having a good time?

All: Yeah.

•   •   •

Reporter: Can you describe the Mall of America in one word?

Woman 1: Wonderful!

Woman 4: Big. Real, real big!

Man: Outstanding!

Boy 1: Fun!

Boy 2: Good!

Women: Great!

•   •   •

Reporter: And that's the way it is, here at the Mall of America. This is Neil Murray saying, Why don't you come and see for yourself?

13 At the state fair

Various people enjoy a day at the fair.

Steve: Oh, corn on the cob, I love that. We always had that at the fair when we were little.

Liz: We did, too.

Vendor 1: Hey, this is the place! Get your fresh corn on the cob here! Fresh, hot-roasted corn on the cob! . . . What would you like?

Steve: I'll have one of those, please.

Vendor 1: Coming up. . . . What about you? Would you like one, too?

Liz: Not right now, thank you. I'm not hungry.

Steve: Maybe you should give us another one, anyway!

Vendor 1: Sure.

• • •

Nancy: Oh, he is *so* cute!

Rick: Yeah, but that was a lot of work. Now let's find a place to eat.

Betsy: How about over there? There's a restaurant where we can sit down, too. My feet are tired. . . . You can keep the dog with you.

Rick: Oh, all right. (*to stuffed dog*) Come to papa, yeah. Aw, good boy. Yuh!

Waitress: Hi! May I take your order?

Betsy: Yeah, I think I'll have a hot dog and a small order of french fries.

Waitress: Would you like anything to drink?

Betsy: I'll have a small diet cola.

Waitress: OK. And what can I get for you?

Nancy: I guess I'd like a salad plate and a cup of tea, please.

Waitress: What kind of dressing would you like on that?

Nancy: Do you have Thousand Island?

Waitress: Yes, we do. Would you like anything else?

Nancy: No, that'll be all, thanks.

Waitress: Thank you. And how about you?

Rick: A hamburger, a large order of fries, and a chocolate milk shake, please.

Waitress: Anything else?

Rick: How about something for our little friend?

• • •

Paul: I'm glad that's over.

Cynthia: I'm hungry. How about you?

Paul: I don't know. I don't think so.

Cynthia: Oh, look! They're selling ice-cream cones!

Vendor 2: Hi. What'll you have?

Cynthia: I'd like a cone, please.

Vendor 2: How many scoops?

Cynthia: Three, please.

Paul: Three scoops?

Cynthia: Yes, one for me and two for you!

Vendor 2: Thank you.

Cynthia: See, I knew you wanted some.

14 Around the World: the game show

Marlene, Jack, and Kathy are contestants in a game show.

Announcer: And now it's time to play "Around the World" with your host Johnny Traveler.

• • •

Johnny: Ladies and gentlemen, welcome to "Around the World," the game show about world geography. And now, let's meet our players.

Announcer: A computer engineer from Seattle, Washington, Marlene Miller! A high school teacher from Boston, Massachusetts, Jack Richardson! And from Vero Beach, Florida, an accountant, Kathy Hernandez!

Johnny: Welcome to "Around the World." And now, let's begin our game. Our categories are Deserts and Mountains, Rivers and Waterfalls, Oceans and Islands, Cities and Countries. Marlene, please begin.

Marlene: I'll try Rivers and Waterfalls for fifty, Johnny.

Johnny: Which is longer, the Nile River in Africa or the Amazon River in South America? . . . Jack?

Jack: Um . . . um . . . the Nile.

Johnny: That's right for fifty! Next category, please.

Jack: OK, I'll try Deserts and Mountains for fifty, Johnny.

Johnny: Which is higher, Mt. McKinley in North America or Mt. Kilimanjaro in Africa? . . . Marlene.

Marlene: Mt. McKinley.

Johnny: That's right. Your category, please, Marlene.

Marlene: I'll take Cities and Countries for fifty, Johnny.

Johnny: What country is sometimes called the "island continent"? . . . Kathy.

Kathy: Australia!

Johnny: That's right for fifty. Your category, please.

Kathy: I'll take Deserts and Mountains for one hundred, Johnny.

Johnny: What is the largest desert in Asia? . . . Jack.

Jack: Oh, I know the answer. It starts with G. . . . Go . . . Go . . . Gobi!

Johnny: Yes, the Gobi Desert! Wonderful! You have one hundred points. The next category, please, Jack.

Jack: Cities and Countries for a hundred.

Johnny: What is the largest city in North America? . . . Kathy.

Kathy: New York!

Johnny: No. Good try. . . . Jack.

Jack: Uh . . . Los Angeles?

Johnny: No. Sorry, Jack. Marlene.

Marlene: Mexico City.

Johnny: That's right for one hundred. Your category, Marlene?

Marlene: I'll try Rivers and Waterfalls for one hundred, Johnny.

Johnny: Angel Falls is the highest waterfall in the world. What country is it in? . . . Jack.

Jack: Uh . . . Brazil.

Johnny: No. I'm sorry, Jack. . . . Kathy.

Kathy: Uh . . . Colombia!

Johnny: No, that's not correct, Kathy. . . . Marlene.

Marlene: It's Venezuela, Johnny.

Johnny: That's right! You have one hundred points. Next category, please, Marlene.

Marlene: Oceans and Islands for fifty, Johnny.

Johnny: Ooh! That's the end of our game. Let's look at the score. Hey, it looks like Marlene has won. Congratulations, Marlene.

Marlene: Thanks, Johnny.

Johnny: Now, let's see what you've won.

Announcer: Marlene, you've won tickets for two on Countryside Airlines, the friendliest airline in the sky, to one of the most exciting, beautiful, fascinating cities in the country . . . Seattle, Washington!

Marlene: But I live in Seattle, Washington!

Johnny: Ooh. . . . Well, that's our show! Until next time, I'm Johnny Traveler for "Around the World"!

15 May I speak to Cathy?

Cathy's father is trying to work, but the phone keeps ringing.

Mr. Waite: *(Phone rings.)* Hello?

Kevin: Hello, may I speak to Cathy?

Mr. Waite: I'm sorry. She's not in just now.

Kevin: Is she coming back soon?

Mr. Waite: Uh, yes, I think so.

Kevin: Well, could you tell her that Kevin called and that I'll call back later?

Mr. Waite: Sure, Kevin.

Kevin: Thank you. Good-bye.

Mr. Waite: Bye. . . . *(Writes message.)* Kevin will call back.

• • •

Mr. Waite: *(Phone rings.)* Hello?

Jenny: Hello, Mr. Waite. This is Jenny. Is Cathy home?

Mr. Waite: Oh, hi, Jenny. No, Cathy's not here right now.

Jenny: Will she be back soon?

Mr. Waite: Uh, I'm not sure. Would you like to leave a message?

Jenny: Well, could you just tell her to call me when she comes in?

Mr. Waite: Sure, I'll tell her. Bye, Jenny.

Jenny: Bye, Mr. Waite.

Mr. Waite: *(Writes message.)* Call Jenny.

• • •

Mr. Waite: *(Phone rings.)* Hello?

Rachel: Hi, this is Rachel. Is Cathy home?

Mr. Waite: Uh, no, she's not, Rachel. Would you like her to call you when she comes in?

Rachel: Yes, please. She has my number.

Mr. Waite: I'll tell her, Rachel. Bye.

Rachel: Bye.

Mr. Waite: OK. *(Writes message.)* OK. Call Rachel.

• • •

Cathy: Hi, Dad. I'm home!

Mr. Waite: Hi, Cathy.

• • •

Cathy: Have there been any calls for me?

Mr. Waite: Just a few! Kevin called. He'll call back. Jenny called. She wants you to call *her*. And then Rachel called. She wants you to call her, too.

Cathy: Great!

Mr. Waite: The messages are next to the phone.

Cathy: Oh, OK. . . . *(Phone rings.)* I'll get that. . . . Hello? . . . Uh, no, actually he's busy right now. . . . Oh, OK. I'll call him, then. . . . Dad, it's your boss. He said it's urgent.

Mr. Waite: All right. I'm coming.

Cathy: Just a moment. He's coming.

• • •

Cathy: Dad, are you all right?

Mr. Waite: I'm OK. I'm OK.

Cathy: Just a moment.

• • •

Mr. Waite: John speaking. . . . Oh no, no! Uh . . . no problem! No problem at all!

120

16 A whole new Marty

Marty changes his image and makes new friends.

John: I'm just terrible at calculus. I don't understand anything in this chapter.

Marty: I know what you mean. It is a tough course.

John: Did you figure out the answer to this problem?

Marty: That's in Chapter 11. I did that last week. Let's see.

Michelle: Hi, John. I see you're working on calculus.

John: Oh, hi, Michelle. Yes, I am. Michelle, you know Marty, don't you?

Michelle: Yeah, hi, Marty. Say, John, I've got a couple of questions about Chapter 12. Do you want to study together?

John: Well, uh, actually, I'm still on Chapter 11, but Marty here is working on Chapter 12.

Michelle: Oh, that's OK. Actually, I've got to go to class right now. See you later.

John: OK, Michelle. See you.

Marty: Gee, John, how do you do it?

John: What?

Marty: Girls. They always talk to you. They never even notice me.

John: That's not true.

Marty: Yes, it is. Listen, I need some advice.

John: Well, maybe you could cut your hair. And your clothes . . . I don't know. They could be a little neater.

Marty: I see what you mean.

John: You need to be more outgoing. Maybe you should exercise. Then you'd have more energy.

Marty: Well, when do we start?

John: Well, how about right now?

Marty: OK. Sounds good to me.

• • •

Michelle: Hi, John. How are you?

John: Oh, hi, Michelle.

Michelle: Do you want to study together for the calculus exam?

John: Well, actually, I have to study for my history exam right now. But maybe Marty has some time.

Marty: Hi, Michelle.

Michelle: Marty?

Marty: Yeah.

Michelle: I didn't recognize you! There's something different about you. Did you change your hairstyle?

Marty: Well, it's a little shorter.

Michelle: Hmm, maybe that's it. Well, anyway, would you like to study for the calculus exam?

Marty: Sure. No problem. When do you want to start?

Michelle: How about right now?

Marty: OK.

John: Looks like Marty has a new friend.

What is American food?

People try to figure out what American food really is.

Reporter: Hello. Are you feeling a little hungry? I am. And there certainly are a lot of different kinds of food to choose from here: . . . Japanese, . . . Mexican, . . . Italian, . . . and maybe even . . . American, whatever that is. My name is Jennifer Santoro, and I'm here to find out what people in the USA like to eat. I'll be asking a lot of questions, and I may even get some good answers to a very difficult question: What is American food?

California-style restaurants, like this one, are found all over the United States. These restaurants are known for their interesting use of fresh fruits and vegetables. You can see the influence of many international cuisines, for example, Mexican, . . . Japanese, . . . and Italian. Let's find out what people say about eating here.

• • •

Reporter: What did you have for lunch today?

Man 1: I had a chicken salad.

Reporter: And what's your favorite kind of restaurant to eat in?

Man 1: Uh, I like these California restaurants.

Reporter: What did you have for lunch today?

Man 2: Uh, I had a Caesar salad.

Reporter: So, what are you eating for lunch?

Woman 1: Uh, pasta.

Reporter: How often do you eat out in restaurants?

Woman 1: Quite often, in Taiwan.

Reporter: How often, once a week, twice a week?

Woman 1: Almost every day.

• • •

Reporter: Almost every town and city has at least one Chinese restaurant. This one is in a neighborhood shopping center, and it's well known for its lunch buffet.

• • •

Reporter: What are you eating today?

Woman 2: I'm having Chinese food.

Reporter: What's your favorite kind of food?

Woman 2: I really do enjoy Chinese.

Reporter: How often do you go out to eat?

Woman 2: I go out several times a week, usually four or five times for lunch.

Reporter: What are you eating?

Man 3: I'm having, uh, hot-and-sour soup and Kung-pao chicken.

Reporter: What's your favorite kind of food?

Man 3: Well, I enjoy Chinese food. I enjoy most foods, I guess.

Reporter: How often do you go out to eat?

Man 3: Oh, probably five, six times a week, minimum.

Reporter: What are you having?

Woman 3: I'm having the pork Szechwan, which is one of the specials of this restaurant.

Reporter: What's your favorite kind of restaurant?

Woman 3: I like this restaurant.

• • •

Reporter: Sometimes in America you can mix a little music and food together, such as in this German-style restaurant.

• • •

Reporter: So what did you have for lunch today?

Woman 4: I had, um, a salad, and I also had goulash, Bavarian goulash, which was very good.

Woman 5: I had the, uh, German . . . uh . . . cabbage, and the, uh . . . German potato salad, . . . and it was excellent.

Man 4: I had a German bratwurst.

• • •

Reporter: In all of the restaurants we visited, we asked people what they thought was a typical American food.

Man 2: I think it's very much hamburgers and french fries.

Woman 6: Pizza.

Woman 1: Hamburger, hot dog.

Man 5: Steak.

Man 6: A typical American food would be . . . ah . . . french fries, hamburger, hot dogs . . .

Woman 2: Hamburger and french fries.

•   •   •

Reporter: This restaurant specializes in typical American hamburgers and french fries . . . and the fast service many Americans like. . . . What are you having?

Woman 7: Um, I'm having a hamburger, and french fries, and a Coke.

Man 7: I think I'm going to order the hamburger, . . . cheeseburger, maybe.

Woman 8: I'm having a cheeseburger, fries, and a Coke.

Man 8: Uh, hamburger.

•   •   •

Reporter: So, what is American food? One answer is . . . hamburgers! But as we've seen, American food is really a lot of good things to eat from all over the world. . . . I'm Jennifer Santoro, and now, I'm going to eat!

Authors' Acknowledgments

A great number of people assisted in the development of both the original *Interchange* Video 1 and *New Interchange* Video 1. Particular thanks go to the following:

The **reviewers** for their helpful suggestions:

Valerie A. Benson, Julie Dyson, Dorien Grunbaum, Cynthia Hall Kouré, Mark Kunce, Peter Mallett, Pamela Rogerson-Revell, Chuck Sandy, and Jody Simmons.

The **students** and **teachers** in the following schools and institutes who pilot-tested the Video or the Video Activity Book; their valuable comments and suggestions helped shape the content of the entire program:

Athenée Français, Tokyo, Japan; **Centro Cultural Brasil-Estados Unidos**, Belém, Brazil; **Eurocentres**, Virginia, U.S.A.; **Fairmont State College**, West Virginia, U.S.A.; **Hakodate Daigaku**, Hokkaido, Japan; **Hirosaki Gakuin Daigaku**, Aomori, Japan; **Hiroshima Shudo Daigaku**, Hiroshima, Japan; **Hokkaido Daigaku, Institute of Language and Cultural Studies**, Hokkaido, Japan; **The Institute Meguro**, Tokyo, Japan; **Instituto Brasil-Estados Unidos**, Rio de Janeiro, Brazil; **Instituto Cultural de Idiomas**, Caxias do Sul, Brazil; **Musashino Joshi Daigaku**, Tokyo, Japan; **Nagasaki Gaigo Tanki Daigaku**, Nagasaki, Japan; **New Cida**, Tokyo, Japan; **Parco-ILC English School**, Chiba, Japan; **Pegasus Language Services**, Tokyo, Japan; **Poole Gakuin Tanki Daigaku**, Hyogo, Japan; **Seinan Gakuin Daigaku**, Fukuoka, Japan; **Shukugawa Joshi Tanki Daigaku**, Hyogo, Japan; **Tokai Daigaku**, Kanagawa, Japan; **YMCA Business School**, Kanagawa, Japan; and **Yokohama YMCA**, Kanagawa, Japan.

The **editorial** and **production** team on the original or revised classroom video and the accompanying print materials:

Sarah Almy, Suzette André, John Borrelli, Will Capel, Mary Carson, Karen Davy, Andrew Gitzy, Deborah Goldblatt, Deborah Gordon, Stephanie Karras, James Morgan, Kathy Niemczyk, Chuck Sandy, Kathleen Schultz, Ellen Shaw, and Mary Vaughn.

The **editorial** and **production** team on *New Interchange* Level One: Suzette André, Sylvia P. Bloch, John Borrelli, Mary Carson, Natalie Nordby Chen, Karen Davy, Randee Falk, Andrew Gitzy, Pauline Ireland, Penny Laporte, Kathy Niemczyk, Kathleen Schultz, Rosie Stamp, and Mary Vaughn.

And Cambridge University Press **staff** and **advisors**: Carlos Barbisan, Kate Cory-Wright, Riitta da Costa, Peter Davison, Stephen Dawson, Peter Donovan, Cecilia Gómez, Colin Hayes, Thares Keeree, Jinsook Kim, Koen Van Landeghem, Carine Mitchell, Sabina Sahni, Helen Sandiford, Dan Schulte, Ian Sutherland, Chris White, and Ellen Zlotnick.

And a special thanks to the video producer, Master Communications Group.